TRADITIONAL
HOME BOOK OF
H·E·R·B·S

TRADITIONAL
HOME BOOK OF
H·E·R·B·S

MICHAEL JANULEWICZ

TODTRI

DEDICATION

For Juliana

This book was designed and produced by
Todtri Productions Limited
P.O. Box 572
New York, NY 10116-0572
Fax (212) 279-1241

Printed and bound in Singapore

ISBN 1-880908-40-9

Author: Michael Janulewicz

Publisher: Robert M. Tod
Designer and Art Director: Ron Pickless
Editor: Nicolas Wright
Typeset and DTP: Blanc Verso/UK

CONTENTS

INTRODUCTION

*Talk of perfect happiness or pleasure, and what
place was so fit for that as the garden place where
Adam was set to be a herbalist.*
GERARD

Every garden brings its own delight to its gardener, usually in equal measure to frustration, and disappointment too. Herb gardening is no different, but personally more rewarding than growing prize roses or chrysanthemums. This book is about herbs more than gardening, and I trust this will not disappoint too much. I hope that the seasoned gardener will find new ideas and new things to try, but equally that the new gardener will discover the joy of growing herbs for their own sake.

There are many facets to the fascination of herbs - first, they are useful in so many ways, from food to cosmetics and medicines, but they are also a living link with human history. The fact that most garden herbs are little changed from the wild species and have been collected and cultivated for thousands of years, means that this link is continuous and direct. The very names conjure up a past that we can only otherwise capture in books and the nature of the often fanciful claims to the efficacy of herbs plunges us into a magical world before the scientific age.

The motto of the American Herb Society adequately sums up what herbs are to today's gardener - 'For use and delight'. And both come true with a little care and effort.

Michael Janulewicz

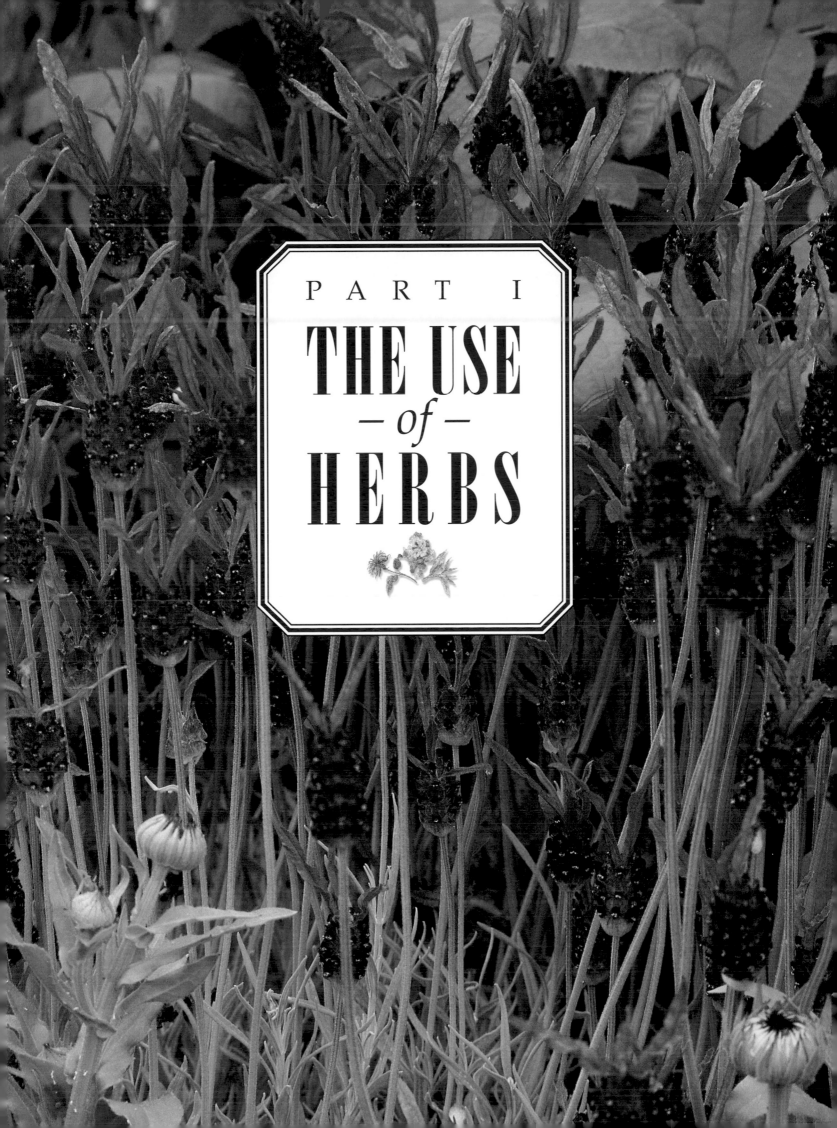

PART I

THE USE
– of –
HERBS

A SHORT HISTORY OF HERB GARDENING

Above: 'Six bunches a penny, sweet blooming Lavender' was one of the historic cries of the street traders of London. All kinds of herbs were brought from the country to be sold in street markets up until World War II.

Opposite: The Chelsea Physic Garden, London, England: Founded by the Society of Apothecaries in 1673, the Chelsea garden remained in the hands of the apothecaries until the turn of the century and is little changed. The herbs are grouped according to their uses for example culinary, medicinal and dyeing.

With no written records of early human societies we cannot be sure when plants were first cultivated in what we would recognize today as a garden. Archaeological evidence, however, does show that early humans relied on plants for clothing, food and medicine and it is probably safe to assume that the most valued plants were transplanted from the wild to be cultivated closer to the protection of home.

The first written records appear in Egypt, Assyria and China and the fragmentary evidence shows that plants were extensively used as medicines with well over two hundred drugs being prescribed. With the flowering of the Classical Age in Ancient Greece and Rome we find extensive records from 300 BC to the latter half of the first century when Pliny the Elder listed more than a thousand plants in his work *Historia naturalis*.

The Romans introduced plants to, and collected them from, every corner of their Empire. Yet still there is no evidence that the plants were ever regarded as anything more than useful, and ornamental gardening, as opposed to raising crops, probably did not exist in a formal manner, other than in the houses of noblemen. With the fall of the Roman Empire many of the conquered lands returned to their local folk beliefs in plants, but within the Christian monasteries of Europe the more scientific tradition was upheld, with gardens full of medicinal and food plants laid out within the grounds.

Meanwhile, the Islamic encroachment through North Africa and eventually into Spain by the seventh century saw Arab scholars continuing the Greek tradition and discipline of science.

The importance of plants to sustain communities was never lost. At the coronation of Charlemagne, leader of the Holy Roman Empire, in 800, it was decreed that a list of eighty-nine plants should be grown in every city. But still the understanding of plants and medicine was based on the Greek and Roman orthodoxy until the European Renaissance of the seventeenth century.

In 1439 there was one event that changed the world. When Johannes Gutenberg developed movable type and the printing press, information about the world was suddenly available to

more people, more quickly and more cheaply. Although the Bible was the first printed book, a collection of Herbals soon followed and we owe virtually all of our historic knowledge of gardening to these early editions, although most were still based on translations — often very bad translations — of the original Greek texts.

With the discovery of the Americas more and more plant material was available and the traffic in plant stock and seeds was regarded as of prime importance and a potential source of wealth and power. Potatoes, tomatoes and tobacco were some of the earliest imports and now regarded as almost natives. Yet at the same time the first formal gardens were being laid out, mostly geometric patterns of hedges of such plants as box, thyme and cotton lavender. These were filled in with plants to complete the pattern - a style that reached the height of its popularity in Elizabethan knot gardens, its zenith in the great parterres of Versailles and its nemesis in Victorian carpet bedding, unfortunately still practised by town and city landscapers today.

Above: A tempting display of culinary herbs in a French market garden.

Opposite: Plimouth Plantation, MA: The reconstructed houses and gardens of the early colonial period show how herbs were grown in raised-bed kitchen gardens.

Yet although recognizable as gardens for aesthetic pleasure, the plants were merely building material to create shapes and uniformity was the byword. These patterns have, however, come down to us as the true historic herb garden and copies of famous knot gardens and designs for new ones are still a valid option for today's gardener.

Developing in parallel were the first botanic gardens. The first, set up in Italy in the 1540s at Pisa and Padua, grew herbs to service their schools of medicine. The idea spread across Europe, first through Italy then northwards to France, the Netherlands and England — the first 'Physick' garden being set up at Oxford in 1621. By this time Gerard, the great English herbalist, had published his *Herball*. These gardens were laid out in ordered plantings, maybe grouping plants of similar use together such as medicinal, dyeing, culinary. The formality of these plots also offers a true version of the historic herb garden.

With the advent of the natural landscape gardening movement, led by William Kent and Capability Brown, flowers were virtually banished from the garden. Nature now came right up to the walls of the house. The great formal gardens were swept away and herbs and other flowers relegated to the kitchen garden. And there they stayed until the Victorian fashion for architectural bedding schemes which lasted in many gardens to well into the twentieth century.

The English writer William Robinson published his book *The English Flower Garden* in 1883, generally attacking what he saw as the blandness and superficiality of Victorian carpet bedding. Along with his adherent Gertrude Jekyll, they virtually re-invented the concept of the cottage garden, with herbaceous plants being valued for their own individuality and how they could be combined to create an overall effect. Gardening took off in this new direction and is very much what we still find today. That many of the re-discovered cottage garden plants were herbs, with their uncomplicated flowers and forms, brings us back to the earliest forms of gardening.

Opposite: Raised beds in a kitchen garden.

WHAT IS A HERB?

Opposite: Nasturtiums and pot marigolds mix gloriously with alliums and chervil showing how annuals can lend a splash of color to the herb garden.

Below: Lavender growing wild in the Mediterranean.

The boundaries of what defines a herb are are both vague and varied. To the technically minded botanist a herb is a plant that has a herbaceous habit, one than dies down in adverse conditions such as winter or excessive heat and grows again the following season. For annuals this means setting seeds, for other there is some form of storage organ such as a bulb or other rootstock. To the herb gardener this definition is too narrow and it would be nonsense to believe shrubby herbs

such as rosemary or bay cannot be classified as herbs.

For the herb gardener it is safe to use the definition that if the plant is useful in some way — for food, medicine, or dyeing for example — then it is a herb. This expanded, and sensible, definition allows us to include virtually every form of plant — shrubs, perennials, biennials, annuals, shrubs and even small trees such as the bay. And within these forms they come in a kaleidoscope of colors and shapes of flower, different leaf patterns, spreading habits, mat-like groundcover, tall plants, short plants and a variety of seeds and fruits. They can be evergreen or deciduous, fragrant or not.

THE ECOLOGY OF HERBS

The herbs we grow today are virtually the same plants grown by our ancestors. While plant breeders expended time and energy developing bigger, better and longer-lasting flowers in an ever-increasing palette of colors, the more humble and practical herb plants remained unaffected. The aim for the herb gardener, then, is to reproduce the natural habitat of the wild plants. Many, such as sage, rosemary and thyme come from the Mediterranean and to thrive need sun, a free-draining soil and a semblance of protection from cold winds. Others such as angelica and woodruff are natives of woodlands and will tolerate partial- or full-shade. Others such as bergamot seem happy in most conditions if they are not too extreme.

If you have a loose free-draining soil you will have few problems, but heavy clay will need to be broken up by digging in grit and compost. A soil that is too dry needs well rotted manure or compost to give it body — but not too much as an over-rich soil promotes leggy, sappy growth at the expense of flowers and flavor in the leaves. Most herbs are forgiving and will thrive if treated fairly harshly.

Cold winds are particularly detrimental to shrubs such as rosemary, bay and lemon verbena and all will need a permanently sheltered spot, or preferably moved indoors to a greenhouse or conservatory during winter. Other than that most herbs need only a regular watering if the weather is dry and regular weeding to reduce competition, but most importantly do not ignore them. Herbs, like people, enjoy company and are much happier for it.

Above: Topiary box lends a geometric character to the herb garden.

LOW-GROWING HERBS FOR PATHS
Chamomile
Creeping savory
Pennyroyal
Shepherd's thyme
Woodruff

Opposite: Bergamot, a North American native that has adapted to most countries and most soils.

Previous page: Chamomile lawns release a sweet apple scent when trodden on. They are, however, quite difficult to maintain.

CHOOSING YOUR HERB GARDEN

A wagon wheel design is a traditional geometric shape for the herb garden, planted with culinary herbs.

Few of us are lucky enough to be able to choose the exact garden site we want. Generally, we inherit them with the home we choose and make do as best we can. Yet every garden, whatever its size and shape has room for herbs and they can even be grown indoors or in a window box if you live somewhere without a garden.

Although space may be a limiting factor, the real decision is whether you wish to have a formal or informal herb garden before you begin planting. The rules of good garden design apply equally to a herb garden as to any other form of gardening. The gardener has to pay attention to soil type and aspect to decide what will thrive and what will struggle. Planting plans taking into account the height, habit, color and flowering time need to be worked out on paper first before transferring the design to the real garden. If you only wish to plant a garden with a theme such as culinary or medicinal herbs the overall effect makes a big difference to the final appeal of the garden.

But because herbs are there to be used, plants there is a need to be able to get close to them for harvesting or simply enjoying the varied scents that they produce. To this end there are some basic rules and traditions that can be applied to the herb garden and once the framework is established the plantings become purely a personal choice.

PATHS AND STEPPING STONES

Herbs and natural stone, or old bricks and tiles, go particularly well together and make the many herbs that hail from the rocky Mediterranean regions look more at home. Paths and stones are also practical, allowing access to the herbs even in wet weather. And aesthetically the hard lines of a path are joyfully softened

HERBS FOR SHADE OR PARTIAL-SHADE

Angelica
Bergamot
Chervil
Lemon balm
Lovage
Mint
Sweet cicely
Woodruff

Sundials and statuary make excellent focal points for both a formal and informal garden.

Paving slabs can create a practical, geometric herb garden.

Right: Knot gardens, with the framework patterns made of clipped hedges, can be constructed on a small scale.

Below: Parsley, chives and oregano find a home in an old pair of scales. Using unusual containers adds interest to the herb garden.

by plants that tumble over the edges. If you want to keep a deep informal effect, set stepping stones among the plantings or small brick paths that meander through the bed.

Bricks and stoneware can also be used to define the shape of a garden. Cartwheel, chequer board and ladder herb gardens are popular and classic designs. They are also practical, for the brick or tile divisions and keep the spreading plants such as mint in bounds.

Shingle or gravel paths also work well with most herbs and even using it as a mulch throughout the planting can work to good effect. It also has the added advantage of keeping down annual weeds and conserving moisture.

HEDGING HERBS

These herbs can be clipped into tallish hedges to protect the herb garden or as part of geometric design.

Lavender
Rosemary
Southernwood
Wormwood

FEATURES

Traditional stone features such as sundials, fountains and urns create a focal point if placed in the center of the garden. They add height and visual interest, drawing the eye into the garden. Any piece of statuary, or even old chimney pots planted with trailing plants, will have the same effect. But while stoneware can be expensive, added interest can be given by planting standard roses or clipped bay trees.

Terracotta pots can be used indoors or out and suit most herbs.

HERBS SUITABLE FOR GROWING IN POTS INDOORS

Culinary

Basil
Bay
Chervil
Chives
Marjoram
Mint
Parsley
Savory, winter
Tarragon
Thyme

Ornamental

Lemon verbena
Pineapple sage
Rosemary

Right: A kitchen garden in July, planted out with leeks, chives and sage.

Opposite: Benches in gardens allow the gardener a well earned rest to enjoy the fruits of his or her labor. Here thyme, basil, parsley, tarragon, sorrel and chives are ready for the kitchen.

Height can also be introduced by training climbing herbs up wrought iron frameworks or an arch of trellis to create small arbors at the entrance to the garden.

Garden seats and chairs are available by the dozen - in wrought iron and natural and painted wood. A seat placed close to the scented plants is a good idea and, or preferably a planting arranged around the seat, to enjoy the summer fragrances.

GARDEN DIVISIONS

An enclosed herb garden adds an air of control to the plants and creates a kind of intimacy, rather like the privacy of a

A traditional herbaceous border with cotton lavender, feverfew and lavender.

Lavender, fennel, chives and purple sage create a good composition.

special room in the house. Brick walls, hedges or some kind of solid fencing covered with climbing plants can all be employed to build the garden's framework. Low hedges of cotton lavender, lavender, or box can all help to define specific areas of the garden and even an edging of chives can add form to an otherwise uncontrolled planting.

GROWING HERBS IN CONTAINERS

If you only have a small garden, or just a patio or even no garden at all there are still opportunities for growing herbs in pots and other containers and in window boxes. Most herbs will grow successfully in pots, and for half-hardy ones such as bay, lemon verbena and pineapple sage which need some form of winter protection, being able to move them is an advantage. Tall, deep rooted herbs such as fennel or angelica do not, however, make successful pot-grown specimens and their height even makes them look out of place.

The choice of container is up to you. Traditional terra-cotta pots always look good and stone troughs and old sinks can be used for a neatly contained garden. Plastic pots, now looking exceptionally good imitations of the real thing, have the advantage in that they are lighter so making it more easy to move plants about. Half-barrels, chimney pots and old milk churns can all be improvised as a container and add a rural quality to the herb garden. Always be on the look out for different kinds of container to add interest.

The rules for successful herb growing in pots is the same as for any pot-grown plant. Good drainage, good compost, regular - but not over - watering and feeding are all essential.

And when the herb has outgrown its home it will have to be repotted into something bigger. Window boxes and hanging baskets dry out much more quickly than the garden or pots and in dry weather need to be watered every day. And anything grown on a window sill should be turned regularly to ensure that growth is equal on all sides of the plants as it grows towards the light.

Whatever your final choice of garden, remember that not everything always goes to plan. Some herbs will thrive, others will struggle, some may have to be sacrificed to make room for others.

Remember that a garden is a living thing and not only changes with the seasons but also with the years and as long as you are adaptable the garden will respond and grow with you.

PLANNING THE GARDEN

The ground rules for planting a herb garden are the same as for any garden.

• Measure the site and transfer the dimension to paper, squared graph paper is ideal.

• Plan your plantings, taking into account the color, flowering time, height and spread of the herbs you choose.

• Lay out the plan in the garden, using string and canes or by dibbling lines of sand or earth for the dividing lines.

HERBS FOR EDGING

The following plants are suitable for edging along a front of the garden or bed as their height does not obscure the other plantings

Basil
Catmint
Chervil
Chives
Clary sage
Cotton lavender
Curry plant
Feverfew
Hyssop
Lavender
Marigolds
Marjoram
Parsley
Rue
Savory
Thyme

USING HERBS

Herbs are not only attractive garden plants, they are also by definition useful plants, and many have long traditions in cooking, medicine, cosmetics, perfumery and dyeing. The following pages describe many of the ways in which herbs can be used today. All are achievable with little effort and need no more than ordinary household equipment.

Herb vinegars are easy to make and good to use. These are basil and garlic salad, burnet, tarragon and dill and garlic vinegars.

CULINARY HERBS

The great bridge between the cook and the gardener is the herb garden, providing fresh ingredients for every occasion and myriad different flavors. Whether you are roasting, garnishing, stewing, stuffing, baking bread, biscuits or cakes or fruit pies and jellies and jams, herbs gathered fresh from the garden will always add something special.

Although herbs were first grown for medicines and to disguise the bad flavors of many foods, particularly meat, by the sixteenth century they entered the cuisine of most countries. Today a regular and wider choice of fresh foodstuffs has made herbs more popular than ever, and as an added bonus they can

Opposite: A delightful array of fresh herbs provide an endless variety of tastes in the kitchen.

Above: Cooking with herbs adds an extra flavor to the dish. Here is brochette of fish with herbs, halibut salad and baked halibut with rosemary.

Left: An al fresco delight – Ruchetta al Funghi.

Opposite: Herbs in olive oil.

Above: Tomato and mozarella with basil, the traditional Italian accompaniment to tomatoes.

be used to enliven the dull texture of much processed food and add valuable nutrients.

WHERE TO START

There are some culinary herbs that must be regarded as essential and these include basil, bay, chives, marjoram, mint, parsley, rosemary, sage, tarragon and thyme. All are easy to grow and most are happy growing in pots, sinks or tubs if space is limited. An extended list to include angelica, borage, chervil, coriander, fennel, hyssop, lovage, sorrel and both summer and winter savory will provide the kitchen with virtually all it needs. But do not be restricted by convention, experiment with different herbs and tastes to suit you and your culinary ambitions.

Most herbs are best fresh as the volatile oils in their leaves that produce their distinctive flavor and aroma evaporate when they are dried. Take them from the garden as you need them. Use sharp scissors to cut herbs rather than chopping them on a wooden surface as the wood will absorb some of the flavor. The golden rule with herbs is not to use too many. They are supposed to augment the taste of the food not take it over and

Opposite: Oils and vinegars with herbs and fruit – not only a useful collection but a visually enticing display.

Overleaf: Herbs, with added spices, in olive oil.

HERBS FOR FLAVOR

From the basic culinary herb garden most herbs are used as flavorings and go best with certain foods.

Basil Eggs, meat, tomato
Caraway Carrot, cabbage, pork, salads
Chervil Chicken, fish, eggs, pulses
Chives Eggs, cheese, tomato, green salad
Dill Fish, eggs, pickles, vegetables,
Fennel Fish, salads, soup
Hyssop Pork, salads
Lemon balm Fish, chicken
Lemon thyme Fish, chicken
Lovage Chicken, salad, stews, soups
Marjoram Fish, meat, tomato, potato
Mint Lamb, peas, potato
Parsley Fish, chicken, potato, soup
Rosemary Lamb, chicken
Sage Pork, duck, onion
Savory Beans
Sorrel Salads, soups
Tarragon Chicken, fish, tomato, vegetables
Thyme Meat, fish, chicken, vegetables

FINE HERBES AND BOUQUET GARNI

Fines herbes is a finely chopped mix of tarragon, chives, chervil and parsley which should be added to a dish just before serving, acting as a seasoning and garnish. Bouquet garni is used to flavor soups and stews and consists of three sprigs of parsley, two of thyme and a bay leaf tied together. After the dish has cooked the herbs are discarded.

many a meal has been ruined by the belief that more is better. Add small quantities at a time until the flavor is to your liking. Remember that dried herbs have a more pungent — but different — flavor from fresh herbs and you will need less of them.

Try new ideas and combinations of herbs as there are no hard and fast rules. There are, however, traditions about which herbs combine best with which food and are worth noting. Some are concerned with flavor, others to make the food more easy to digest or as substitutes for salt and sugar. It is hard to imagine the English table without mint sauce with lamb, Italian tomato dishes without basil or the French without a bouquet garni in the stewing pot. Every recipe book you have will give its own recommendations.

HERBS FOR THE BAKERY

Bread has traditionally been flavored with the seeds of caraway, dill and fennel and occasionally with the sweeter seeds of anise,

Above: **Crystallizing herb flowers makes them suitable for decorating cakes.**

Previous page: Herb quiche in a pastry case.

Opposite: Fresh mint vinegar.

caraway and coriander more usually used for cakes and biscuits. Caraway is, however, often used in rye bread.

Marigold petals, chopped or whole can be added to cakes, sweet buns or scones while in Roman times small cakes containing seeds of anise were handed to guests at the end of a meal to help digest the previous courses - a custom that has been suggested is the tradition of the wedding cake. Modern wedding cakes with a profusion of dried fruits and sugary icing will, however, probably have the opposite effect. Another traditional cake in England was the tansy cake eaten at Lent, bitterly flavored with the juice from the leaves or chopped leaves themselves.

For decorating cakes, crystallized borage flowers and mint leaves, or candied angelica stems add colors that look natural when compared to the modern artificial colorings available. Herb sugars can be made by adding fresh leaves of mint, peppermint or lemon verbena to sugar for sweetening or decorative icing.

Sealed in a jar the sugar absorbs the flavor as the leaves dry out. Anise sugar is used in the making of petit fours and for sugar-free fruit pies angelica will reduce the tartness of acidy fruit.

HERB EXTRAS

At the opposite end of the taste spectrum, herb salts can add special interest to a meal, either in the cooking or as a condiment. The method is the same for any herb, depending on your taste, but lovage, chives and basil work well. Use plain salt to make a bed in a baking tin, place a layer of herbs on it then cover with another layer of salt. Bake in a moderate oven for twenty minutes, stirring after ten. When the herbs are crisp it is ready for sieving into an airtight container.

For the less health conscious, herb butters and cheeses add a welcome change to all kinds of dishes. Mix in a tablespoon of finely chopped herbs to two ounces (60gm) of butter, creaming well before adding a tablespoon of lemon juice. If you lack a dairy for full-scale cheese production, cottage cheese mixed with basil, tarragon, sweet cicely, chervil, chives, parsley or sage - alone or in any combination to suit your taste - will provide a satisfying variety.

For condiments, herb mustards and jellies can be made from your chosen herbs. For mustards try parsley, sage, tarragon, marjoram or lovage, for jellies mint, rosemary and marjoram or even lavender.

HERB VINEGARS

Making your own herb vinegars for salads, dressings or sauces is easy. Tarragon is the most versatile but chives, dill, basil, fennel, marjoram, mint, salad burnet and thyme all have their place in the kitchen. Take two good handfulls of the herb just as they come into flower and bruise the leaves. Place them in a jar and cover with three pints (1.8l) of white or red wine vinegar. Malt vinegar is not suitable as the herbs struggle to overcome the malt taste. Leave the mixture to infuse for a few weeks, tasting it regularly for flavor. When it is ready strain the liquid into a jar or bottle and add a sprig of the fresh herb before stoppering the container.

EDIBLE FLOWERS

Some herb flowers are safe to eat and can be added to salads and desserts for decoration.
Borage
Nasturtium
Hyssop
Marigold

Left: The edible garden includes pot marigolds, nasturtiums, and pineapple sage, calendula and salvia.

HERB TEAS

TEA HERBS

Although many herbs can be used to make teas, not all of them are suited to modern tastes. The following are palatable and are made from more or less the most popular herbs

Angelica Colds and coughs – *Leaves, stems, seeds and roots*
Anise Digestion, colds and catarrh – *Seeds*
Bergamot Refreshment – *Leaves*
Borage Refreshment, fever – *Leaves and flowers*
Calamint Refreshment – *Leaves*
Caraway Indigestion – *Seeds*
Chamomile Headaches –*Flowers*
Coriander Stomach and colic – *Leaves and seeds*
Costmary Relaxation – *Leaves*
Dill Indigestion – *New leaves and seeds*
Feverfew Headaches – *Leaves*
Lemon balm Refreshment and flu – *Leaves before flowering*
Mint Digestion and nausea – *Leaves*
Parsley Kidneys – *Leaves and stems*
Rosemary Headaches and colds – *Leaves and flowers*
Sage Sore throats and gums – *Leaves*

Herbal teas, or tisanes, as substitutes for the more usual drinks of tea and coffee, with their high caffeine content, are becoming more popular than ever. You can buy them pre-dried, pre-packed and pre-packaged in a little bag with a piece of string attached, but there is nothing more enjoyable than fresh herbs gathered from the garden or the ones you have dried yourself. Most herbal teas were originally brewed for their curative, relaxing or stimulating properties, and many still form the basis of commercially produced medicines.

Herb teas can be drunk either hot or chilled and iced for a refreshing summer drink. Adding honey as a sweetener can take the edge off some of the more tart tastes and lemon juice can add a little zing where necessary. Leaves, seeds, roots and flowers of different herbs can all be employed by the teamaker, and there are two basic methods - infusing or simmering. The golden rule is never to use metal containers, only ceramic ones and the silver rule is to have a teapot cover at hand as herbs need longer to infuse than ordinary Indian and China tea.

A full handful of clean fresh leaves, or a teaspoon of dried, per cup is usually adequate. Pour on the boiling water and leave for five to seven minutes to suit your taste before straining. Some herbs such as bergamot, lemon balm and pineapple sage may need to be simmered for up to ten minutes to release their full flavor. For seed-based teas of anise, dill, fennel, coriander and lovage a half teaspoon of crushed seeds per cup is usually enough.

Many herbs blend well together so experiment with different flavors to find the tea that suits your palate best. Equally, bergamot, lemon balm and lemon verbena can be added to ordinary Indian tea to create a new experience.

Right: Angelica growing with calendula and lettuce.

WINES, BEERS AND OTHER DRINKS

TRADITIONAL FLAVORED WINES

Maibowle is a traditional German summer drink.

Add a handful of dry woodruff to a bottle of dry white wine and cool in the refrigerator for four hours. Add wild strawberries and a bottle of soda water before serving.

Hippocras is made from spiced grape wine, honey and the herb of your choice, but rosemary and marjoram work well.

Dissolve 1lb (450g) of honey in a pint of water, adding half a lemon and a spice such as cinnamon or cloves and a handful of the herb of your choice. Allow to cool and add two bottles of red or white wine. Stand for four hours and strain before serving.

It was probably by happy accident that prehistoric humans first discovered that wild honey mixed with water and left for a while would produce a drink with enough alcohol to relax them after a hard day hunting and gathering and bring some comfort to an unheated cave. Centuries of human curiosity saw different flavors being added and herbs were the main source even if the alcohol was derived from a different base.

The first beers pre-date the Roman Empire, brewed from a mixture of grain mashes and flavored with such herbs as

Right: Hops have been used to give a distinctive bitter taste to beer for more than five hundred years.

Opposite: Garden mint is the flavoring of choice for mint juleps.

The cucumber-flavored leaves and starry blue flowers of borage are ideal additions to summer drinks.

costmary, also called alecost, and clary sage which was said to make you 'dead drunke, or madde drunk'. Clary wine became the great aphrodisiac of the sixteenth century, and you can still make muscatel sage wine clary by adding the flowering tops to wine from your local wine shop. Mugwort was another approved additive for beer. It was brewed from the dried flowers, or innkeepers would place some leaves in a mug and pour beer over them while the thirsty customer waited for the taste to infuse. Eventually hops became the flavoring of choice, although not without resistance from the traditionalists. In England, Henry VIII was petitioned to ban hops as 'wickede weedes that wille spoile the taste of drinke and endanger the peoples'.

Today, many commercial alcoholic drinks derive their unique taste from herbs. Anise flavors pastis, ouzo and arak, coriander is used in gin manufacture, liquorice gives Guinness its distinctive sweet-bitter taste, the traditional liquers such as Chartreuse contain a special blend of herbs known only to the monks who

HOMEMADE PARSLEY WINE

1lb (450g) fresh parsley
2lb (900g) sugar
1 gallon (5l) of water
teaspoon of all-purpose yeast
4oz (125g) raisins
Rind and juice of 2 lemons
and 2 oranges

Boil parsley and fruit pool-ings for 20 minutes, strain and stir in chopped raisins and sugar. Allow to cool and add fruit juice and yeast. Ferment until ready.

make it, mint is unmistakable in creme-de menthe and borage flowers remain an ingredient in Pimms.

For the home winemaker the herb garden supplies suitable starting materials. Parsley, angelica and lemon balm leaves produce interesting and palatable white wines and the flowerheads of marigolds make something interesting but somewhat variable. Other herbs can be employed to flavor wines that you buy, especially if they are of a doubtful pedigree, so experiment with lemon balm, lemon verbena, mint, rosemary, clary sage and other sages and dried sweet woodruff. Mint with bourbon makes the legendary mint juleps.

Borage, however, is the queen of drinking herbs. Flowers and flowering tops added to red and white wines seem to 'cool' them, and they are the essential ingredient for summer cups, punches and non-alcoholic fruit drinks for their flavor and stunning decoration. Mint, and both lemon balm and lemon verbena, also are a refreshing addition to a homemade summer punch.

THE
SCENTED GARDEN

HERBS WITH AROMATIC LEAVES AND FLOWERS

Angelica
Anise
Basil
Bay
Bergamot
Calamint
Chamomile
Costmary
Cotton lavender
Curry plant
Hyssop
Lavender
Lemon balm
Lemon verbena
Lovage
Marjoram
Melilot
Mint
Rosemary
Sage
Pineapple sage
Southernwood
Thyme
Woodruff
Wormwood

Opposite: A heady mixture of scents – an irregular chamomile path between herb beds and lavender edgeing.

Of all the senses, smell is the most evocative, capturing and recapturing moments in time that neither sight nor sound can. Roses and jasmine may produce strong heady scents, but they are short-lived. By contrast, many herbs carry their distinctive scents for longer as it is mostly the leaves that contain the volatile oils rather than the flowers. Hot sun draws them out and brushing past rosemary, mint or lavender fills the air with instant aromatic surprises. Just squeezing a leaf between finger and thumb opens up a wide spectrum of distinctive smells - the sharp lemon of lemon balm, lemon verbena or lemon thyme, the subtle minty shades between spearmint, peppermint and pennyroyal, the sweetness of lavender and rosemary, the pungency of marjoram and thyme and the freshness of anise and wormwood.

If you have decided on planning a scented garden it is wise to ensure that the plants are close to paths or the front of beds to benefit from their full effect. A rosemary bush planted near a door so you brush by it works well. Also consider planting fragrant plants around a garden bench or seat, so the scents waft upwards or run your hands through the foliage to release the perfume. Lavender and wormwood, for example, grow easily to hand height. Or go the whole way and build a chamomile seat that releases its sharp apple smell when you sit on it.

A chamomile lawn, although an attractive idea, is generally impractical unless you have time to maintain it, and anyway grass does a better job in most gardens. A small patch of chamomile in the path, however, will produce the same if somewhat diminished effect. Shepherd's or Corsican thyme or pennyroyal will also sit snugly in cracks in paving and survive being trodden on.

There are many scented herbs to choose from, but as with culinary herbs where individuals tastes vary, so it is with smell, the most complex of our senses. What smells delightful to one person, is sickening to another. While it is easy to describe the scent of some herbs - appley, orangey, lemony or pineapple for example - others defy verbal description and 'balsamy, pungent, spicy, oily' can mean diferent things to different people. Before you decide on your planting scheme take a trip to your local garden centre and nose your way through.

HERBS FOR THE HOUSE

In times past, scented herbs were brought into the house to disguise the unpleasant smell of the rather insanitary living conditions. Some such as woodruff, hyssop and tansy were strewn on the floors and replaced regularly, while others such as lavender carried their scent for months when dried. Lavender is still popular and easy to use. When the spikes are fully in flower cut them, bundle them up and hang them to dry in a warm dark place. When fully dry it is simple to strip the flower heads off the stems and store them in airtight containers.

A mixture of blue glass and pot pourri is a feast for all the senses.

Place some in an open bowl and as the scent fades replace them with new flowers from your store. Do not waste the old stems and flowers as added to an open fire they release a heavenly if short-lived perfume.

It is the essential oils held in plants, in either the leaves, stems or flowers that yield the perfume. Commercial perfumes are distilled from these oils, but although full-scale perfume manufacture is beyond the scope of most herb gardeners, the essence can still be captured in making pot pourris.

Pot pourris are a mixture of dried flowers and leaves. Collect them on a dry day, but early enough before the sun has begun to evaporate their essential oils.

Dry each herb separately and store them in airtight containers. As different herbs flower or are at their peak at different times of year, over a growing season you will build up a collection of ingredients. If you want to add color to your pot pourri then collect flowers from other parts of the garden. Rose petals are almost a must, but geraniums, jasmine, violets and delphiniums add visual variety.

There are three more things you will need - powdered orris root to fix the fragrance, some cinnamon, nutmeg or allspice from the kitchen and commercially available flower oils such as rose oil. Take about two pints (1l) of mixed leaves and flowers, a tablespoon of orris root, a teaspoon of mixed spices and a few drops of your chosen oil and mix them thoroughly in a bowl. You can put the mixture in open bowls around the house, but the scent fades quite quickly and it is usual to keep them covered, removing the lid to release the scent at certain times of day or on special occasions.

Pot pourris can be mixed from many different herbs and the art is to create a mixture that gives you fragrance and pretty colors.

INSECT REPELLENTS

Many herbs that are pleasantly scented to us have the opposite affect on insects. Pennyroyal, for example was traditionally kept in beds to repel fleas and bay leaves in a kitchen cupboard drive away silverfish, although the same claim for cockroaches seems farfetched. Moths certainly fall prey to cotton lavender, lavender, costmary, tansy, southernwood, wormwood, tansy and mugwort. A mixture of these dried herbs put in small bags and placed in drawers and wardrobes not only deters the insects, but also adds a refreshing fragrance.

HERBS FOR POT POURRIS

Flowers
Bergamot
Borage
Chamomile
Lavender
Marigold

Leaves
Angelica
Basil
Bay
Bergamot
Costmary
Lavender
Lemon balm
Lemon verbena
Marjoram
Mint
Pineapple sage
Rosemary
Southernwood
Thyme
Woodruff
Wormwood

Fresh or dried herbs give a flower arrangement
a feel of the country.

HERBS FOR FLOWER ARRANGING

DRIED HERBS
Ambrosia
Clary sage
Cotton lavender
Lavender
Marjoram
Tansy
Wormwood

FRESH HERBS
Ambrosia
Angelica
Basil
Borage
Chamomile
Cotton lavender
Elecampane
Feverfew
Hyssop
Lavender
Marigold
Marjoram
Rosemary
Rue
Southernwood
Tansy
Woodruff
Wormwood

The great variety in the color, shape and form of the foliage and flowers of herbs add a valuable string to the flower arranger's bow, with the added bonus that many of them are strongly fragrant. Because most herbs have hardly changed from their original wild form, unlike so many garden plants that have been bred and improved for centuries, they lend a natural air to an arrangement and set off the bold, some may say brash, cultivars with covergirl blossoms.

Anyone who has picked wildflowers for their delicate beauty will know that they wilt rapidly when in the house, some having gone over before they reach home and there is nothing you can do to revive them. The herbs described here will capture that outdoor natural look and survive well indoors when cut. In many countries it is illegal to pick wildflowers at all, and if not the practice should be discouraged anyway.

Right: A delicate posy of borage flowers.

Opposite: Terracotta and glass containers show off to the full a display of parsley, lovage, marjoram, basil, lemon balm, bay and feverfew.

MEDICINAL HERBS

The first recorded written prescription has been found on a 2000-year-old Egyptian papyrus, but even before this plants from the fields and forests were gathered to cure sickness, heal wounds and stimulate health. The Greeks and Romans began to catalogue herbs and list cures, although medicine was still entwined with magic and astrology. During the so-called Dark Ages the monks of the great monasteries of Europe became keepers of the herbal tradition, but the link with astrology carried on well into the nineteenth century.

As more natural healing methods became popular, such as the *Doctrine of Signatures* - which was based on like curing like where red flowers were good for blood and heart-shaped leaves would treat the heart - so the literature grew and the accumulated claims became more wild. And as new plants were being sought out and returned to Europe from all over the world so the available material increased in volume. Protection from lightning, mad dogs, witches, the plague, seeing in the dark and recognizing fairies were all available.

Today, herbalism, homeopathy and aromatherapy as complementary medicines still rely on herbs that grow in our gardens and many modern drugs such as aspirin and quinine derive from plants. Many cough, cold and indigestion remedies contain natural plant extracts, especially mint. Eczma, a successful treatment for which has eluded modern drug and conventional medicine, can be helped by infusions of mixed Chinese herbs.

Many plants are, however, poisonous and it is not recommended that anyone should take anything without proper medical advice. Satisfy yourself with herbal teas for headaches, sore throats, indigestion and colds, and costmary and comfrey leaves to rub on bee stings and insect bites. Small cuts can be staunched with the dried powdered roots of bistort or the leaves of salad burnet and marigold, which may be a more attractive option than tissue paper for the haphazard shaver. Dried marigold petals infused with water or made into an ointment is a good surface healer of cracked skin and grazes.

Relief from aches and pains can be achieved by massaging with herb oils - peppermint for muscles, rosemary for headaches and lavender for aching joints. Grind enough herbs in a mortar and fill a small jar with them. Add a tablespoon of white wine vinegar and sufficient almond oil to cover the herbs. Keep the jar in a warm place, shaking regularly, straining off the herbs after three weeks.

Compresses of comfrey and hyssop leaves can reduce swellings and draw bruises and the antiseptic qualities of thyme and sage make them an efficient gargle for sore throats and gums. Chewing the leaves of feverfew has been a reliever of headaches since Elizabethan times and is currently being seriously investigated by commercial pharmaceutical companies who will hopefully also improve the taste.

Many claimed cures seem fanciful, but a handful of hops under a pillow may help an insomniac, although it is doubtful that 'ashes of southernwood and salad oil' will cure baldness.

Jars of herbal remedies, a basket of buds and a mortar and pestle – a few herbalist neccessities.

COSMETICS

HERBS FOR THE BATH

Angelica
Basil
Chamomile flowers
Costmary
Lavender
Lemon balm
Lemon verbena
Lovage
Marjoram
Mint
Mugwort
Pennyroyal
Rosemary
Sage
Thyme

Natural beauty products are available commercially everywhere, and are more popular today than ever. The ingredients come from all over the world and creams, oils, shampoos, bath oils and the like are concocted from all kinds of exotic fruits, barks and leaves. Yet among them our own garden lavender, rosemary, chamomile and thyme still hold their own.

Full scale perfume manufacture is an impossibility without specialized equipment. There are, however, various bath waters, hair rinses, and shampoos that can be made at home.

For fair hair use chamomile flowers, for dark hair rosemary flowers. Add a teaspoon of dried chamomile flowers or a 4in (10cm) sprig of rosemary to a cup of boiling water and leave to infuse until cold. This can be used as a final rinse or added to a

Dried chamomile flowers make a hair rinse for blonde hair, always keeping it light.

Sage – a herb with many cosmetic uses.

final rinsing water. Lemon verbena and lemon balm also make a good fragrant rinse, neutralising the skin after shampooing or soaping. Toilet vinegars can be made in the same way as culinary vinegars, lavender being the most useful. Added to the final rinsing water it will have a stimulating effect on the scalp. Lavender vinegar can be added to washing water, too.

Shampoos of southernwood and sage can also made with little effort. A tablespoon of fresh leaves should be infused in two pints (1l) of water and simmered for about fifteen minutes. Allow this to cool slightly and strain the infusion onto small pieces of pure unscented soap, stirring to dissolve it completely. The resulting mixture can be stored in stoppered bottles and used like any other shampoo.

For an instant herbal bath for relaxation or stimulation, and improved skin and circulation there are many herbs to choose from. Place a handful of herbs in a muslin bag and tie it under the hot tap as the water runs. Alternatively, the herbs can be infused in two pints (1l) of boiling water for fifteen minutes and the infusion strained into the bath. Angelica, lovage and mugwort not only acts as a skin tonic but also as a deodorant.

Try dried herbs in different combinations putting them into muslin bags that can be hung in the water to infuse while you relax. It should not be long until you find the right mixture to suit your moods and needs.

HERBS FOR DYEING

Tansy is one of the traditional dyeing plants, yielding a yellow or orange dye.

Plants produced virtually all dyeing material before the invention of chemical dyes. These, however, became more popular because they were easy to manufacture, held faster and were more consistent and sharper in color. That is not to say that vegetable dyes are still not used commercially throughout the world and there is a revival of interest in the more subtle colors that they can produce.

Producing your own dyes is unfortunately a time-consuming process, but is an enjoyable and absorbing hobby none-the-less if you have the patience and the willingness to experiment. All kinds of plants yield dyes, not just those we classify as herbs, and many wild and wayside species such as dandelion, *Taraxacum officinale*, which produces a magenta color, can easily be collected. Some carry the dye in the leaves and flowers, others in their berries and seeds and others in their roots.

Some natural dyes are still used for traditional purposes. The little-grown madder, *Rubia tinctorum,* has for centuries been used to produce the brilliant red of cardinals' hats and cloaks, although it can also be persuaded to yield purple, orange and yellow. Woad was the blue body paint of the Ancient Britons and although no doubt it was designed to terrify the invading Romans it has been suggested that it was also used to help heal any battle scars as it is a natural styptic.

DYEING AT HOME

For the home dyer there are a few basic principles of to follow. Use only raw wool, anything that has been bleached will not work. Thoroughly wash the wool in hot, but not boiling, water with soap but never detergent, simmering it for at least an hour. The purist would choose to use the soap from the soapwort here. Allow to cool, and rinse out the soap.

The next stage is to add what is known as a mordant - this is essential for the dye to take to the wool and helps hold the color fast. You can make your own from a mixture of alum and cream of tartar, but it is best to look for a commercially available mordant and ask advice from your supplier. Two hours of simmering the wool in the mordant should be sufficient to fix it.

Finally, take the vegetable dye material, chop it up and put it in a muslin bag in about four gallons (18l) of water for about

DYER'S HERBS

Madder	Crimson
Marigold	Yellow
Tansy	Yellow/Orange
Woad	Blue

ten hours. Boil until the color is the shade you require, but remember that the finished product will be lighter. Add the wool and gradually heat, simmering until you have reached the desired color. Wash out excess dye and dry away from direct sunlight or heat.

It is important to use soft water if possible, and never use cooking utensils as the residues of many plants can be poisonous. Rubber gloves will stop you getting green fingers - in the house at least.

A yellow dye can be extracted from the petals of marigold.

THEME GARDENS

With so many different herbs to choose from, and many being amenable to most gardens, where do you start? If you want herbs to cook with, the choice is one that matches your tastes and ambitions. You can design a formal or informal garden, grow the plants for fragrance, for flower arranging, drying, medicines or to make teas as we have seen. But there are endless other ideas, some of which are suggested here. There is no limit - except for your imagination.

WILDLIFE GARDENS

The silent beauty of butterflies and the murmuring antics of bees and other flying insects add an essential element to every

BEE HERBS
Bergamot
Borage
Catmint
Comfrey
Hyssop
Lavender
Lemon balm
Marigold
Marjoram
Melilot
Mint
Rosemary
Sage
Savory
Thyme
Woad

HERBS FOR BUTTERFLIES
Catmint
Hyssop
Lavender
Marjoram
Marsh mallow
Rosemary
Soapwort
Thyme

Right: Bees attracted to the garden help to pollinate other plants.

Opposite: Butterflies find many herbs irresistible and thyme is one of the favorites.

Opposite: A constant source of ideas – Chelsea Physic Garden with the statue of Sir Hans Sloane gives many designers the inspiration for themed gardens.

Below: Artemesia – a fine example of white and silver garden display.

garden, animating an otherwise still place. Many herbs are irresistible to fervent foraging bees and even the more languid butterflies can be attracted into the herb garden by planning your planting. Obviously other flowers also attract insects but you may choose to incorporate them into a wildlife garden. A bird bath or bird feeders strategically placed complement the natural attraction of herbs in enlivening the garden.

WHITE AND SILVER GARDENS

Choosing a one- color planting scheme can be a dramatic addition to a bed or corner. White is a favourite as the flowers show up in the evenings as darkness closes in. Silver and white foliage plants such as wormwood and cotton lavender can be

used to set the framework and filled in with white flowers or seeded plants such as woodruff and chervil. Again, you can mix in other plants such as white roses, white violets, bleeding heart, lily of the valley and Solomon's seal to extend the flowering season. There are white varieties of many plants and a scan through a comprehensive nursery catalogue will help you find out what is available.

LITERARY OR HISTORICAL GARDENS

For the literary minded a collection of herbs mentioned in the plays and sonnets of Shakespeare draws up an authentic Elizabethan garden. Adding old-fashioned cabbage, damask and musk roses complements the herbs perfectly. The garden could be informal or perhaps an Elizabethan knot garden, edged with box. There are many other literary themes that can be explored with a little research - the Bible is a popular theme - but why not try your favourite poet or author?

Other historical themes can also make interesting topics. Why not a Roman garden, as the Roman Empire introduced plants throughout its range from Africa to Great Britain? The restoration of the gardens at Colonial Williamsburg, Virginia provides essential material for early American gardens. And later the Shakers who left Liverpool, England to settle in Albany, New York in 1774, became the great upholders of the herb tradition, their self-sufficiency in medicine making them eventually the suppliers of medicinal plants, seeds and extracts throughout the continent. By the early 1800s they were collecting more than two hundred native plants from the wild and cultivating forty from European imported stock. Checking Shaker community records will give you a list of the plants they grew.

A WITCH'S GARDEN

Herbs, as ancient cultivated plants, have featured in thousands of myths and belief in witchcraft led to many claims that they were essential ingredients of spells. It is not a coincidence that these plants are deadly poisonous and produce extremely powerful drugs.

If you do plant a witch's garden make sure they are labelled clearly and they must be kept away from children at all cost. That said they are all interesting plants. Henbane, *Hyoscyamus niger*, is the classsic ingredient of witches' brews, monkshood, *Aconitum napellus*, is so poisonous that there is no known antidote and hemlock, *Conium maculatum*, was used to kill the Greek philosopher Socrates in 399BC. Opium poppy, *Papaver somniferum* - perhaps the best of the ornamental poppies - is the source of pure opium. Mandrake, *Mandragora officinarum*, with its roots that resemble the body of a human, is reputed to scream when pulled from the ground.

For those afraid of witches, marigolds, southernwood, ivy, *Hederaelix*, and the dried leaves of St John's wort, *Hypericum perforatum*, can keep them from entering the house. No doubt they work as no witches have been to tea at my house since I planted the southernwood!

HERBS WITH WHITE FLOWERS AND SEEDS
Caraway
Chervil
Coriander
Melilot
Sweet cicely
Woodruff

HERBS WITH SILVER/GREY FOLIAGE

Cotton lavender
Curry plant
Lavender
Mint
Sage
Southernwood
Thyme
Wormwood

SHAKESPEARE'S HERB GARDEN

Bay
Chamomile
Fennel
Hyssop
Lavender
Marigold
Mint
Marjoram

Opposite: Shakespeare's border in Stratford-upon-Avon, England. Recreating historic gardens from literary references is one way of forming a herb collection.

HARVESTING AND STORING

HERBS FOR DRYING

Basil
Bay
Borage
Chervil
Chives
Dill
Fennel
Hyssop
Lemon Balm
Lovage
Marjoram
Mint
Parsley
Rosemary
Sage
Salad burnet
Savory, winter and summer
Tarragon
Thyme

A still life display of sage, rosemary, bay, dill, garlic and onions

There is no substitute for herbs gathered fresh from the garden to embellish a dish, but not all herbs are available fresh all year round and storing them by drying or freezing ensures a supply over the lean winter months. Drying for fragrance for pot pourris, flower arranging or decoration is another string to the herb gardener's bow.

The art of preserving herbs is to capture the essential oils that give them their flavor or fragrance as quickly as possible. This also means harvesting them at the time of day and stage of the growing cycle when they are in their greatest concentration.

A marjoram posy.

TIME OF DAY

Gather herbs in the morning, after the dew has dried, but before the sun is at its hottest when the essential oils begin to evaporate. As you will want clean leaves, stems or flowers it is useful to hose the plants the night before to clear away the dust and dirt. The time of year is rather more complicated and varies from herb to herb.

Obviously if you are collecting flowers you need to wait until they are open. If collecting seeds you must wait until they ripen. For leaves they are at their best when the flower buds have not formed but before they open. Chives is an exception and can be trimmed and used whether in flower or not. After flowering the quality of the leaves deteriorates, sage is a particular offender.

Try to handle the harvest as little as possible to avoid bruising the leaves and releasing the oils. Use a sharp knife or a pair of scissors to cut the herbs cleanly.

For annuals such as basil and summer savory, make regular cuttings, trimming back to above a leaf bud to encourage new bushy growth.

It is possible, with a little planning, to gain three crops in one growing season. For perennial herbs the most you should cut back is about two-thirds of its height. This should encourage a second bushy growth for a harvest later in the year. However, heavy harvesting in this way destroys much of the attractiveness of the plant as an ornamental and if you do want large quantities of a particular herb it is much better to keep some plants in the vegetable garden.

The aim of drying herbs is to retain the color and essential oils by driving off the moisture. For this you need warmth and good ventilation to take away the moisture, the entire operation preferable being undertaken in the dark as sunlight destroys the color and reduces the essential oil content. Place the collected herbs on a newspaper on a tray, spreading out the individual elements so they do not touch. A temperature of about 86°F (30°C) is ideal, anything significantly lower takes too long, anything much higher will dry too quickly. Luckily, an airing cupboard provides the right conditions of heat, ventilation and darkness. It is possible to dry herbs in a low oven or even a microwave, but the results are variable and you will need to experiment quite a lot with getting it right.

When collecting seeds, cut the flower head with a length of stem and place them upside down in plain paper bags. Hang these in a dry well-ventilated place until the seeds begin to drop. A shake of the bag will then release all of the ripe seeds.

STORING DRIED HERBS

Herbs should be kept in airtight containers and stored in the dark to keep their flavor This may be less attractive than a display of herb jars in the kitchen, but you can have the best of both worlds by filling the jars from your store as you need them. After a year most dried herbs lose their flavor so they are best discarded and replaced with a current year's crop.

FREEZING HERBS

Virtually all herbs freeze well, although many are available all year round fresh from the garden and freezing them seems taking a 'belt and braces' policy too far. Treat them like vegetables, although there is no reason to blanch them if you do not want to. The art is to freeze herbs in small quantities, in useful amounts that you will need for cooking. Defrosting and refreezing gradually damages the plants if you only need a leaf or a small a sprig each time.

Another idea is to freeze selected herbs in ice blocks in an ice tray. Borage flowers and mint leaves for example can be added to summer drinks, ice and all, or a mixture of herbs, such as *fines herbes* can made up and either added to a dish or thawed first.

Finally, remember to label and date your frozen harvest as you would any other vegetable.

SEASONAL HERBS FOR FREEZING

Basil	Marjoram
Chervil	Mint
Chives	Parsley
Dill	Salad burnet
Fennel	Sorrel
Lovage	Tarragon

PART II

A an Z
— of —
HERBS

All the herbs listed here are generally easy to grow and readily available. They include culinary herbs, dying herbs and a range of historical curiosities without which no herb garden is complete. They are ordered by common name, followed by the accepted Latin name. Each herb has a brief description, a guide to cultivation and the uses to which it can be put, both modern and traditional.

You do not have to start at A and finish at Z. Dip in where you like and discover how these humble plants can improve your health and cooking, amuse your cat, drive away moths and even cure baldness.

Angelica: The leaves make a relaxing tea and the stems can be candied as a decorative sweet-meat or stewed with fruits to give them a natural sweetness.

A

AMBROSIA, AMERICAN WORMSEED
CHENOPODIUM AMBROSOIDES

A sturdy bush growing to about 2ft (60cm) high, ambrosia has smallish green triangular leaves and clustered spikes of pale green flowers. Originating in the southwest United States and Mexico, it has a unique flavor and fragrance, producing an unusual fishy smell. Its Mexican name, *Epazote*, translates as bad-smelling animal.

Cultivation
Choose a sunny, well-drained aspect and this herb will mostly look after itself. Sow from seeds or take cuttings, but ambrosia will easily self-seed and can quickly overgrow surrounding plants. Weed out unwanted plants at the seedling stage.

Uses
Cook the leaves with rice, black beans and in soups.

ANGELICA
ANGELICA ARCHANGELICA

Once seen never forgotten. Musky smelling angelica is a strik-ing architectural plant equally at home in the border as the herb garden. It reaches a height of 8ft (2.5m) with large glossy leaves and huge lime-green flowerheads, which resemble cheerleaders' pom-poms, carried on hollow stems.

Cultivation
Botanically angelica is a biennial, growing in the first year, flow-ering in the second and then dying. Start off by buying a plant. It will self-seed freely and you can transplant the seedlings to

the place of your choice. Alternatively, collect seeds from your plant and sow as soon as possible in late summer as they loose their potency with time. Angelica is tolerant of most conditions, but its natural habitat is the woodland and it prefers partial shade with a damp rich soil.

Uses
Candied angelica stems were the traditional green decorations on cakes. Alternatively the young stems can be cooked with rhubarb and soft fruits to sweeten the tartness. The dried leaves make a soothing tea and a good base for a pot pourri.

ANISE
PIMPINELLA ANISUM

Resembling cow parsley with its umbels of white flowers and feathery upper leaves, anise adds little visual interest to the herb garden. It is grown for its aromatic aniseed seeds which are collected as soon as they ripen. Cut down the whole plant and put them in paper bags, or on newspaper, in a warm place to dry.

Cultivation
A native of the Mediterranean, anise needs plenty of sun and a well-drained poor soil to thrive. It is unsuitable for heavy, cold and rich soils and anywhere that does not have at least three months of hot sun. Sow seeds in spring, planting them in blocks as anise has weak stems and tends to flop over if not supported. Thin them to about 8in (20cm) apart.

Uses
Bruised seeds make a tea to aid digestion and whole seeds add flavor to cakes, biscuits, bread and such vegetables as beetroot and cabbage. It remains the basis for alcoholic drinks such as pastis, ouzo and anisette.

B

BASIL
OCIMUM BASILICUM

Basil is the culinary herb *par exellence* and grown for its smooth, oval, glossy leaves that give off a spicy clove-like scent when crushed. It grows into a sturdy bush about 12in (30cm) high and carries spikes of white flowers in mid-summer, but these should be pinched out as they appear to promote more leafy growth.

Cultivation
Sweet basil is a tender annual and needs plenty of sun and a moist soil. Sow seeds in early spring and keep them sheltered

Anise: The small ridged seeds provide a sweet aniseed flavoring.

on a window sill or in a greenhouse. Pot up the seedlings when they are 4in (10cm) tall. Although basil grows happily in open ground it is best-suited to pot growing, either indoors or in a sunny sheltered position outdoors, as growing conditions can be better controlled and the plants are protected from the unwanted attention of snails and slugs.

Uses

Basil and tomatoes complement one another perfectly, and form the basis of most Mediterranean dishes. Use the chopped leaves freely with eggs, aubergines and pasta and basil vinegar as a salad dressing. Always use fresh leaves to retain flavor.

BAY
LAURUS NOBILIS

An evergreen shrub or tree with tough, dark green, glossy leaves that betray its Mediterranean origin, bay is the perfect focus for the herb garden or to stand nobly soldier-like in pots or tubs on patios, decks or near the kitchen door. Under advantageous conditions it can reach 30ft (9m) as a free-growing tree or can be trained and pruned to make standard spirals, pyra-

Bay: Bay trees are either male or female, this is a female in full flower.

mids or globes. Small greenish flowers appear at the base of the leaves in early summer, but a bay tree is either male or female - so unless you have black fruits, it's a boy.

Cultivation

The biggest enemy of the bay is frost and freezing winds. Legions are killed each year. If pot grown they should ideally be moved inside a greenhouse or at least to a protected position. Netting over the foliage gives some protection as does lagging the pots. Propagation is by heel cuttings taken in late summer, but bay is not the easiest plant to propagate unless you have a heated greenhouse or frame. Alternatively they can be layered - pegging down a low branch into the soil, or a pot with a suitable rooting medium, in summer. When rooting is successful the new plant can be detached from its parent.

Uses

The leaves can be used either fresh or dried in soups, stews and casseroles to tenderise the meat and add flavor. Milk puddings take on a subtle taste if a leaf is used during cooking. A fresh leaf placed under a pillow is said to bring inspiration to the sleeper.

Bergamot: The aromatic leaves make a good tea and although usually red-flowered, purple, pink and white is also available.

Opposite: Bistort: Although no longer grown for its vegetable leaves nor its roots for tanning leather, bistort is an interesting inhabitant of the herb garden.

BERGAMOT
MONARDA DIDYMA

A North American native also called bee balm or oswego tea. Growing to about 3ft (1m) it has striking red flowers which last through summer and it is a welcome addition to both herb garden and perennial border. Pink, purple and white varieties are also available. The leaves give off an oily aroma, especially in hot sun.

Cultivation
Bergamot prefers a moist fairly rich soil and will enjoy partial shade. Propagate by dividing the rootstock in early spring.

Uses
Dried leaves are a good base for a pot pourri, the aroma of which is said to clear colds. Hot water pored on a few leaves or flowers makes a delicious, refreshing drink or they can be added to Indian tea to provide a rich, aromatic flavor. It is highly attractive to bees for anyone wishing to increase the wildlife in their garden.

BISTORT
POLYGONUM BISTORTA

A relative of sorrel, bistort is a long-flowering perennial with 2ft-high (60cm) stems carrying spikes of bright pink flowers.

Cultivation
A useful herb for damp areas and half-shade. Propagate by root division in winter or early spring, planting the shoots about 8in (20cm) apart so they can mesh together as they grow.

Uses
Bistort was once an important herb, the leaves being used as a vegetable and the rhizomous roots used in tanning leather. Dried and ground roots were used as flour and to stop bleeding from cuts.

BORAGE
BORAGO OFFICINALIS

The clusters of piercing blue star-shaped flowers are borage's greatest asset, its cucumber-flavored grey-green leaves being rather coarse and covered with bristly hairs. Growing to about 3ft (1m) a single plant can look rather straggly, so plant them in groups of at least three at least 1ft (30cm) apart.

Cultivation
Borage needs little looking after but prefers a moisture-retaining soil and sun. It self-seeds profusely and once you have one borage plant you will have no need to buy or sow seeds for another one.

Borage: The starry blue flowers can be candied or added to summer fruit cups. The leaves have a mild cucumber flavor.

Opposite: Caraway: Although grown for its seeds which are used in cakes, caraway is an elegant addition to the border or herb garden.

Uses

The leaves are a favorite flavoring for fruit cups in summer and the flowers add a delightful decoration. Added to wine, the leaves and flowers were reputed to lift the spirit of the drinker, but the alcohol probably worked just as well. The leaves can be added to salads and the flowers candied. Chopped leaves, lemon and honey are the ingredients for a nightcap tea for a soothing sleep. Borage is probably the best herb garden plant for attracting bees.

C

CALAMINT
CALAMINTHA OFFICINALIS

Calamint – ideal for ground cover.

Suitable for groundcover, calamint rarely reaches 1ft (30cm) in height. Greyish downy leaves with a pepperminty smell set off delicate mauve flower sprays.

Cultivation
Calamint is happy in most situations, but as a flower native to limestone uplands is even happier in a limey soil. Propagate by division in early spring as the new growth begins.

Uses
The leaves make a refreshing tea that was once quite fashionable.

CARAWAY
CARUM CARVI

Grown for its seeds, caraway has feathery leaves that resemble a carrot's, held on elegant 1ft (30cm) stems. The umbels of white flowers set to form brown seeds before the whole plant dies.

Cultivation
Although a biennial, caraway can be treated as an annual. Seeds sown in open ground in spring will not flower until the following spring. Seeds sown as soon as they ripen in autumn will produce flowers the following summer. Thin to about 10in (25cm) apart. When the seeds are ripen, cut down the whole plant and dry them in a well-ventilated place, hung upside down in paper bags. Caraway needs full sun and prefers a good-draining soil.

Uses
Use seeds in bread, cakes, cottage cheese and with cabbage and beetroot. Seeds infused in boiling water were used to aid digestion and for babies with colic.

CATNIP, CATMINT
NEPETA CATARIA, N. MUSSINI

If you want to keep cats out of your garden do not plant catnip, if you love your cat then you can both have hours of fun. The fragrance from the hummock of greyish-green leaves sends cats into a frenzy, making the most elegant and mature cat into a foolish kitten. The purple and white flowers are fairly insignificant and if you desire something more attractive you should plant catmint, *N. mussini*, which has attractive lavender-colored flowers set among grey-blue foliage. It is superb as an edging plant, but cats will still use it to lounge in the sun so it may need some protection.

Cultivation
While happy in almost any soil, both plants need sun. Propagation is by root division, cuttings or seed. Protect young plants and seedlings with netting to save them from the local tom cats.

Uses
Mostly planted for cats, both species are also attractive to bees. Catnip makes a refreshing tea and was once the preferred drink in England before the importation of tea from India. Leaves

Catmint: Loved by bees and cats alike, catmint is a good edging plant and remains an ingredient in cough medicines.

rubbed into meat was a tenderiser and flavorer. Catmint is still an ingredient in cough syrups.

CHAMOMILE
ANTHEMIS NOBILIS

There are several plants that are called chamomile, but this is the perennial version that is grown either for its gold-featured daisy-like flowers or used as a carpeting plant for lawns. Its green lacey foliage gives off a smell of sweet apples when crushed. Chamomile lawns were created where soil was poor and it would stay greener for longer than most grass species. However, to be honest they are a lot of work and grass does the job better in most gardens. A patch in a path or patio is probably the best bet for most gardens and when trodden on releases its distinctive perfume. A lawn of true chamomile will need clipping from spring onwards to prevent it from flowering, so plant the non-flowering variety 'Treneague'.

Chamomile – the perfect scented lawn.

Cultivation

Chamomile is fairly tolerant of most soils, but prefers a light sandy situation. Sow seeds in open ground throughout early spring. Alternatively, increase your plants by root division or detach the young offset plants from the parent in spring.

Uses

The flowers, dried or fresh, can be used as a rinse to keep fair hair fair. A tea from the dried flowers has a relaxing and sedative effect. Chamomile has also been called 'the plant physician' as insects tend to avoid it and when planted near a sickly plant tends to revive it.

CHERVIL
ANTHRISCUS CEREFOLIUM

Chervil is the perfect substitute for parsley and indeed in France and most of central Europe is grown and used as a culinary herb instead of parsley. A hardy annual with tangy light-green feathery leaves, it grows in clumps about 1ft (30cm) high.

Cultivation

A cool, wet climate with limited sun is no problem for chervil. Sow seeds in open ground from early summer in six-weekly successions and again in late summer and early autumn for an all-year-round supply. Chervil will be ready for harvesting within six to eight weeks of sowing, and should be cut before they seed. Most plants will recover and produce another crop.

Uses

Fresh chervil is used as you would parsley, adding flavor to fish and egg dishes and as the base for delicious soups and sauces. It is the key ingredient in *fines herbes*, enhancing the flavor of chives, tarragon and parsley.

CHIVES
ALLIUM SCHOENOPRASUM

A must for the chef whether grown in the herb garden or in pots and containers on the window sill, chives are the Lilliputians of the onion family. They are good as edging plants and if allowed to flower make pretty lilac globes that add a welcome dab of color to the herb garden.

Cultivation

Chives grow well in most situations as long as they have water and preferably sun. Increase your supply by dividing clumps during the dormant period in either spring or autumn. Keep cutting with scissors to promote strong growth, although naturally this will not allow it to flower.

Uses

The delicate onion-flavored stems are chopped and used as a

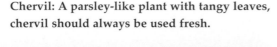

Chervil: A parsley-like plant with tangy leaves, chervil should always be used fresh.

Below: Chives: The leaves make a delicate onion-flavored garnish and if allowed to flower chives are a good edging and border plant. It will happily grow in pots if kept well watered.

garnish for almost everything. They are one of the components of *fines herbes*. The flowers are a favorite of bees and butterflies.

CLARY SAGE
SALVIA SCLAREA

Clary sage is a biennial, producing large foxglove-like leaves the first year and dramatic 3ft (1m) spikes of blue and white flowers surrounded by pink bracts the next. Crushing the leaves releases a fruity aroma, but for the sensitive nose it may be reminiscent of a visit from next door's cat.

Clary sage: The plump spires of blue, white and pink flowers grace any border and on a hot summer's night clary exudes a clean grapefruit-like scent.

Cultivation

A well-drained limey soil and full sun are ideal conditions as long as you water well in summer. Clary sage can swamp smaller plants so is best planted at the back of the herb garden or border. Sow seeds in open ground in spring and thin to about 1ft (30cm) apart. Once established it will self-seed prolifically.

Uses

Wine spiked with clary sage flowers was a renowned sixteenth-century aphrodisiac and the flowers were used as a substitute for hops in beermaking, supposedly making a potent blend that induced drunkenness more quickly. The seeds were used in a potion for cleaning the eyes - clary = clear eye - and the powdered roots taken as snuff to dissipate headaches. The leaves and flowers can be added to jellies or the leaves fried in batter.

COMFREY
SYMPHYTUM OFFICINALE

An ugly duckling that never quite turns into a swan even when it produces its charming clusters of creamy or purplish flowers, comfrey deserves a place in the herb garden for historical reasons - but try to hide its bristly leaves and stems at the back of the garden.

Cultivation

Comfrey tolerates most soil conditions, although it has difficulty with very wet areas and may need watering on very dry days. Propagation looks after itself as it will self-seed aggressively to a point when it becomes an invasive weed rather than a garden specimen. Removing unwanted plants is also a problem as every piece of root is ready to explode into a new plant.

Uses

There has been much debate about comfrey in recent years. At one time it was hailed as the universal plant, providing fodder, food and medicine. Today it is equally damned for containing cancer-forming chemicals. Traditionally, poultices of the crushed leaves were used to treat muscular strains, bruises and to heal broken bones - hence its country name of knitbone. An ointment made from fresh leaves soothes insect bites and promotes the healing of cuts and grazes.

CORIANDER
CORIANDRUM SATIVUM

A spicy herb grown for its seeds and leaves. It is a hardy annual resembling a cow parsley with umbels of mauvish-white flowers.

Cultivation

Sow seeds in open ground in a sunny situation in spring for harvesting in late summer and autumn. As soon as the seeds

have ripened, uproot the plants and hang them upside down in paper bags in a dry place. Threshing the plants will release the seeds. Pick leaves as required.

Coriander: Mostly grown as a crop for its seeds, coriander is a spicy flavoring for curries, meat, cheese, salads and bread.

Uses
Both seeds and leaves are used in a variety of dishes - the leaves in curries and other Oriental recipes and the seeds in sweet and spicy foods.

COSTMARY
TANACETUM BALSAMITA

A 2ft (60cm) perennial with an attractive bluish tinge to its large flat spearlike leaves, costmary has insignificant flowers that fail to impress. Crushing the leaves releases a sweet balsam-peppermint scent.

Cultivation
Choose a well-drained sunny site and costmary will spread by its creeping roots to fill up its surroundings. Root cuttings are the preferred method of propagation. Transplant the new young plants in spring or autumn.

Uses
The plant's alternative name is *alecost* as it was used to brew beer before the introduction of hops in the late Middle Ages. The leaves can be added to salads, stews and soups or infused to make a washing water and to relieve bee stings. Another familiar name is Bible leaf as it was often used as a fragrant bookmark in American churches.

COTTON LAVENDER
SANTOLINA CHAMAECYPARISSUS

Probably the most attractive of the grey/silver-leafed plants available to the gardener, cotton lavender keeps its fragrant foliage throughout winter and is ideal as an edging hedge for a border or formal knot garden. As this shrub is generally clipped to keep its shape, the flowers are rarely seen, but the loss is minimal as the yellow button blooms add little to its effect. For the seaside gardener, they seem to ignore the salt winds.

Cultivation
A Mediterranean native, cotton lavender needs a sunny, well-drained position and will thrive in a poor soil. Although its natural home is in the sun it is remarkably hardy in northern parts. Wet is the big enemy and cold clay soils can send it to the herb garden in the sky. Propagation is easy. Take non-flowering stem cuttings in summer and set them in a suitable rooting medium of equal parts peat and sharp sand. Plant out the following spring. To keep plants in shape, clip twice a year - in spring before the flowerheads appear and again in late summer.

Uses
Historically cotton lavender was used as a cure for ringworm and today is worth adding to sweet bags of lavender, tansy and southernwood as a moth repellent in drawers or cupboards.

CURRY PLANT
HELICHRYSUM ANGUSTIFOLIUM

A perennial shrubby plant with silver-white narrow leaves and small bright yellow flowers. The leaves produce a distinct curry smell when crushed. The curry plant keeps its leaves all year and is a useful edging plant like cotton lavender, but resents being clipped too hard. It can quickly become straggly and will need to be replaced with new plants if it shoots out of bounds. Flowers can be trimmed off before flowering if grown only for its foliage effect.

Cultivation
A free-draining soil and sun are the curry plant's basic needs. Propagate by stem cuttings in late-summer. In winter it can be vulnerable to frost damage and if possible young plants should be protected.

Uses
The curry plant's main use is as an ornamental, but a small sprig added to roast meat dishes does impart a subtle spicy flavor of Indian cooking.

Curry plant: A silver-leaved plant with yellow flowers and a scent of curry from the crushed leaves. Species such as *Helichrysum splendidum* pictured here are more generous with their flowers.

D

DILL
PEUCEDANUM GRAVEOLENS

A 2ft-high (60cm) annual with feathery leaves and flat umbels of green-yellow flowers, dill is grown for its foliage and seeds.

Cultivation
Dill is fast-growing and needs little attention if given a sunny well-drained site. Sow seeds in open ground in early spring as

Opposite: Elecampane: A tall handsome plant now grown as an ornamental, elecampane was once used in monasteries to prevent chest infections and the roots made into sweetmeats.

it is not the best herb for transplanting. For a regular supply of fresh leaves it is best to make successional sowings through until early summer. Pick batches of fresh leaves as required, but if you want seeds it is advisable to wait until the lower seeds are ripe and then cut down the entire plant for drying. Store seeds in airtight containers.

Uses
Fresh leaves can be used in fresh egg and fish dishes or added as a garnish for vegetables. The seeds, which are more pungent, are used to pickle cucumbers and to flavor such vegetables as cabbage, turnips and sauerkraut or added to stews and salad dressings. Dill vinegar is a wonderful accompaniment to fish. A tea from the seeds was formerly used to relieve babies of wind and adults of hiccoughs.

ELECAMPANE
INULA HELENIUM

A traditional herb garden plant grown in monastery and 'cottage gardens' for centuries. Growing to about 5ft (1.5m) it sports dark green leaves and rather raggedy yellow daisy-like summer flowers. It is best grown in clumps at the back of the border or herb garden.

Cultivation
Elecampane is happy almost anywhere except in heavy shade and very dry soils. Sow seeds in pots in early summer for planting out the following spring. Once established, clumps of plants can be lifted in winter and the crowns divided. The Romans used it as a vegetable, medieval monks for a cough mixture and farmers to cure sheep scab, but today it is an ornamental for the 'informal garden'.

FENNEL
FOENICULUM VULGARE

An attractive tall perennial, fennel makes 6ft (2m) at full stretch. The pithy green stems carry delicate feathery green-yellow leaves and flat umbels of small yellow flowers. There is another variety, popularly called bronze fennel, with purple-tinged

leaves which sits comfortably in a mixed border. The bruised leaves release a delicious sweet aniseed flavor.

Cultivation

Fennel is comfortable in most soils and in dry sunny situations. Although it is a perennial, the plant tends to deteriorate over a period of three years and should then be replaced. Sow the seeds in pans in spring and plant out when they are established, although growing-on seedlings in peat pots before they are

Opposite: Fennel: The attractive feathery fern-like fennel furnishes fresh green leaves for the kitchen and seeds for a stomach-settling tea.

Below: Feverfew: Chewing the leaves of feverfew can ease headaches and migraine, but is worth growing for its long-lasting white daisy-like flowers.

transplanted is advisable as fennel resents too much distur-
bance in its youth. Pick fresh leaves as required and collect
seeds as they ripen.

Uses
Fresh leaves enhance any fish dish as a stuffing or garnish
and finely chopped they add a distinctive tang to salads. Add
seeds to cakes and biscuits and as a substitute for dill in
pickles. Fennel tea, brewed from the seeds, was a traditional
method for settling the stomach and dulling hunger pangs.
The Romans believed it to have the power to restore sight
and evil spirits could be kept at bay if it was hung over doors
on Midsummer's Eve.

FEVERFEW
CHRYSANTHEMUM PARTHENIUM

A perennial with strongly scented clumps of green leaves and
pretty white chrysanthemum-like flowers growing to 2.5ft
(75cm) in summer. There is a golden-leaved variety that makes
a vivid splash of color all year round and is often used for carpet bedding with the flowers trimmed off.

Cultivation
Feverfew will grow anywhere except in extremes of wet, dry
and shade. It can be propagated from seed by sowing in trays in
early spring and hardening off before being settled into its per-
manent position. It self-seeds prolifically and unwanted
seedlings should be removed as they appear.

Uses
Since Elizabethan times chewing the leaves and drinking teas
has been used as a cure for headaches and migraine. Today
the idea has come back into fashion and clinical trials are being
carried out by pharmaceutical companies to test the theory.
Grown among beans in the vegetable garden, feverfew will
keep beanfly away.

FLAX
LINUM USITATISSIMUM

An elegant hardy perennial with greyish-green leaves and beau-
tiful blue flowers which reaches a height of 1.5ft (45cm). It is
grown commercially in vast quantities, but for the herb garden
is best regarded as a pretty historical curiosity.

Cultivation
Happy in most soils and situations, but preferring sun, flax is
easily grown from seed sown in trays in early spring for
planting out in summer. Flowers appear the first summer,
improving their productivity for the next two years but the
plant then deteriorates and should be replaced with new
young plants.

Uses
Historically flax provided the fibre for linen, ropes, fishing nets and sacking, but today most of the commercial production is used to extract linseed oil for cattle feed.

Flax: Commercial flax is grown as an annual crop, so for extra color in the herb garden grow the perennial Narbonne flax, *Linum narbonense*, with its magical inch-wide blue flowers.

HEMP AGRIMONY
EUPATORIUM CANNABINUM
JOE PYE WEED
E. PURPUREUM

Britain's native hemp agrimony was formerly grown as a medicinal herb, but is literally overshadowed by its prettier American cousin, Joe Pye weed. Both have rather dull coarse leaves that act as a backdrop to other herbs, but Joe Pye weed can soar to a gigantic 10ft (3m) on rich soils and throws out great plates of purple flowers.

Hemp agrimony.

Cultivation
Both species are happy in a damp soil, preferring part shade although an open site is suitable if you keep them watered. They will self-seed, but this is somewhat random, so propagate by root division when the plant is dormant.

Uses
Used extensively by Native Americans and Shakers alike, Joe Pye weed was named after a well-known medicine man. It was used to treat all kinds of kidney problems and as an ointment and a syrupy tea to cure colds.

HOPS
HUMULUS LUPULUS

Opposite: Hops: Ideal for covering fences or garden buildings, hops are quick growers. This is the golden form 'Aurea'.

A perennial climber that twines itself each year to a height or length of 15ft (4.5m) and is ideal for covering a wire fence or garden outbuilding. The vine-like leaves are green but there is also a golden variety available. Female flowers are carried in

bunches of soft 'cones', while male plants have tiny open sprays.

Cultivation

Most soils and sunny situations suit hops, but they need something to climb and should be directed during the early days of growth in spring. Grown up a wigwam of canes they can add height and interest to any garden, but they can be propagated by cuttings in early spring.

HYSSOP
HYSSOPUS OFFICINALIS

A shrubby plant that grows to about 2ft (60cm) with small dark green scented leaves and delightful spikes of blue flowers that last throughout summer. Lightly clipped in early spring, hyssop makes a good edging plant or internal hedges to divide the herb garden.

Cultivation

A well-drained soil and a sunny position suits hyssop best as it tends to grow leggy if the soil is too rich. Although evergreen, in cold regions or severe winters it can sometimes drop its leaves. For a neat, tidy hedge plants will probably need to be replaced every three or four years. Propagate by sowing seeds in trays in early spring, transplanting them to pots when they are large enough to handle, ready for planting in position in early summer. Alternatively, take some stem cuttings during the growing season, and selecting non-flowering shoots cut at a leaf joint.

Uses

As a culinary herb, hyssop has a strong flavor and should be used sparingly when added to stews, soups, forcemeats and other meat dishes. Finely chopped leaves can lend a strong flavor to salads and the edible flowers used to decorate a salad or sweet dish. Medicinally a tea was believed to relieve coughs and colds and the leaves employed as a compress to draw bruises. Bees find it irresistible.

LAVENDER
LAVANDULA ANGUSTIFOLIA

In a mixed herbaceous border, herb garden or as a low-growing hedge, lavender demonstrates its versatility and is welcome in any garden. Its fragrant silvery foliage and purple flower spikes

Lavender: There is a wide range of lavender varieties available, ranging in height and color from various shades of purple to pale pink and white.

epitomise the country garden. There is now a vast range of different cultivars with varying flower color, shape and size to fit into any planting scheme.

Cultivation
A free-draining soil and a sunny position will see lavender thrive, on heavy clay soils it struggles. New plants can be raised from seed sown in spring, but taking heel cuttings in summer is more reliable. Detach non-flowering shoots with a piece of the old wood attached and pot them in a loam-based potting compost. Regular clipping in spring will keep the plants in bounds as will a second hard cutting in autumn, but after five or six years they become woody and leggy and should be replaced.

Uses
Cut the lavender spikes when in full flower and dry them in paper bags hung up in a warm airy place. The dried flowers

can then be used in pot pourris, in lavender bags as an air freshener or in drawers as a moth repellent. Commercially it is grown for its oil for use in cosmetics and perfumes.

LEMON BALM
MELISSA OFFICINALIS

Rather a Plain Jane of a plant growing to a bushy 2ft (60cm) or more with crinkly oval leaves and small white flowers, lemon balm resembles a cross between a mint and a dead nettle. Its attraction lies in the fresh lemon scent released when the leaves are crushed. Golden and variegated varieties exist and add a little more color to the herb garden.

Cultivation
Grow lemon balm in sun or semi-shade but keep it watered as the roots do not run deep. Propagate by seed, cuttings or root division in spring.

Lemon balm: The sharp lemon-flavor of the leaves makes it ideal for lemon drinks and in cooking wherever lemon is required. It is also an invaluable bee plant.

Uses

A versatile culinary herb, lemon balm is used in forcemeats, salads, mixed with fruit desserts - in fact in almost any recipe when lemon is required. The fresh leaves make a refreshing tea supposed to lift the spirits and ease colds and make a drinkable light white wine. Bees love it and at one time the entrances to hives were rubbed with the leaves to help the bees settle into a new abode. Dried leaves are a good base for a pot pourri.

LEMON VERBENA
LIPPIA CITRIODORA

A native of South America this woody shrub is only half-hardy so it suits a sheltered garden. Even so, if possible they should be overwintered indoors or in a conservatory. In prime sunny conditions it can reach 15ft (4.5m), but usually measures up to a mere 5 or 6ft (1.5-1.8m). The leaves are spear-shaped and the small mauve flowers borne on slender spikes in summer.

Lemon verbena: A woody shrub with lemon-scented leaves, lemon verbena is not always hardy on cold unprotected sites but grows well in a conservatory or indoors.

Cultivation
Take softwood cuttings from the non-flowering shoots in summer, overwintering the plants in a greenhouse or indoors ready for planting out the following spring.

Uses
Leaves picked in summer should be dried for pot pourris or used fresh as an air-freshener indoors or in the car. As an insect repellent it works well in drawers, airing cupboards and wardrobes. In the kitchen a single leaf adds a lemon flavor to rice dishes, cakes and China tea.

LIQUORICE
GLYCYRRHIZA GLABRA

A herbaceous perennial that looks a little shrubby, liquorice has blue-purple pea-like flowers in summer set in the axils of its long pointed leaves. Above ground it makes a good 4ft (1.2m),

Liquorice: An unusual garden plant with purple pea-like leaves in summer. The roots are the source of liquorice for confectionery and commercial medicines.

below ground the roots can sink to 3ft (1m) and run for up to 30ft (9m), throwing up shoots which grow into new plants.

Cultivation
Liquorice likes sun and a moist soil that is well dug and loose if it is to produce its roots to any great extent. Propagate from seed sown in spring in a cold frame, potting up into a peat-based compost when the seedlings are large enough to handle and plant out when established.

Uses
Still a commercial crop, the roots yield the sweet substance used to make all kinds of confectionery, is an additive to some tobaccos and a flavoring in Guinness beer. Medicinally it is added to cough and throat cures and as a stomach settler.

LOVAGE
LEVISTICUM OFFICINALE

Imagine a 6-8ft (1.8-2.4m) celery and you get lovage, and indeed they share a similar flavor and scent when rubbed or crushed. The impressive thick hollow stems carry handsome dark green leaves but unimpressive umbels of greenish-yellow flowers. It is a good background plant in any part of the garden.

Cultivation
Lovage likes a moist rich soil and partial shade but will accept full-sun if watered regularly. Sow seeds in autumn or spring or propagate by root division at the same time.

Uses
Use the stems and leaves of lovage in anything that you would celery. The whole seeds can decorate bread or be ground and added to cake or biscuit mixes. Lovage also has deodorant qualities and an infusion of the leaves was added to their baths by the Romans. This can be achieved at home by tying dried leaves in a muslin bag and placing them under the hot tap when running a bath.

MARIGOLD
CALENDULA OFFICINALIS

An annual grown in cottage gardens for its bright orange or yellow daisy-like summer flowers.

Cultivation
Sow seeds where you want the marigolds to flower. After that

they will self-seed profusely. They are self-sufficient and the only care they need is to be kept weed-free.

Marigold: The golden flowers brighten any garden and the petals, fresh or dried are used to flavor soups, rice, cakes and buns.

Uses
The petals add color and flavor to soups, stews, salads and egg and cheese dishes. It was formerly used as a cheaper substitute for saffron. Medicinally the petals in either a tincture or cream soothe and heal cuts, grazes and chapped skin. Placed on a cut, marigold stops bleeding quickly. The petals also yield an orange dye and are a pretty addition to pot pourris.

Opposite: Wild marjoram: Of all the marjorams the wild species needs the most room to spread as it has a more untidy habit than its cousins.

MARJORAM
ORIGANUM ONITES, O. MAJORANA, O. VULGARE

Of the three culinary marjorams, *O. onites* or pot marjoram, is probably first choice for the herb garden. It is a perennial which forms an 8in (20cm) cushion of green leaves and clusters of mauve flowers. Wild marjoram, *O. vulgare*, is bushier and stragglier, growing to about 2ft (60cm) with hairy leaves and deeper purple flowers. This is the herb oregano and has a more pungent taste than pot marjoram. Sweet, or knotted marjoram, *O. majorana* has the strongest flavor, but should be treated as a half-hardy annual in regions with cold winters. It is, however, happy to grow in pots on indoor window sills. The leaves are smaller and grey-green and the flowers white, growing in 'knots' around the stem.

Cultivation
As Mediterranean natives, all marjorams prefer a sunny position on a light well-drained soil, although both wild and pot marjoram will tolerate partial shade and a heavier soil. Sweet marjoram is propagated by seed, the other two by cuttings or root division in either early spring or autumn. To keep the foliage strong it is advisable to trim back the flowers, although this will disappoint the honey bees who cannot seem to get enough of its nectar.

Uses
Fresh or dry, the leaves are used to flavor forcemeats, soups and stews. Marjoram teas produce a soothing drink and an infusion added to the bath relaxes tired muscles. Add leaves to any pot pourri mixture.

MARSH MALLOW
ALTHAEA OFFICINALIS

Once an important inhabitant of the herb garden and one that deserves to be more popular, marsh mallow grows to 4ft (1.2m) with downy grey leaves and long-lasting pink-purple mallow flowers. At the back of any plot they make an ideal foil to other bright-flowered plants.

Cultivation
Marsh mallow prefers a fairly light free-draining soil to achieve its best growth. Propagate by sowing seeds where you want them to grow or by root division in autumn. It helps to support the early growth with canes otherwise it can easily fall outwards in a circle. After two or three years the plants become unkempt and are best replaced.

Uses
It is the dried root that is used for medicinal and confectionery products. It was once taken as a cure for chest problems, and

used to make the familiar pink and white cushions eaten as candies by children of all ages. Today, sadly, most marshmallows you can purchase have never seen a marsh in their lives! For the kitchen, the roots can be boiled and the shoots chopped into salads.

MELILOT
MELILOTUS OFFICINALIS

A biennial growing up to 3ft (1m) with trifoliate leaves and long spires of yellow pea-like flowers that issue a sweet perfume.

Cultivation
As a clover's cousin, melilot does not like to be moved so sow seeds in early spring where it is to flower. An amenable plant it will tolerate most situations except deep shade.

Uses
Originally used as a fodder crop, it was found to yield antibiotic substances and was used in folk and commercial medicine. The flowers flavor cheeses, tobacco and beer. For today's gardener it is an excellent bee plant and its Latin name translates as bee lotus.

MINT
MENTHA SPP

There are dozens of different garden mints and it is worth growing a few different ones in any garden for their sweet aroma and decorative effect. The pointed-leaved culinary mint, *M. spicata*, is essential for the cook, although Bowle's mint, *M. rotundifolia* 'Bowle's Variety', has a more fruity taste while retaining its pungency in its grey-green thick downy leaves. Peppermint, *M. piperata*, is the one that makes the best tea. Eau de Cologne mint, a variety of *M. citrata*, fills the air with a sweet heady perfume while applemint, *M. rotundifolia*, has fuzzy pale round leaves that smell of fresh apples when crushed. There are also decorative mints such as the ginger mint, *M. gentilis*, which describes its vivid green leaves splashed with gold rather than its flavor. Corsican mint, *M. requienii*, is the smallest mint and suitable for rockeries or as groundcover between paving stones.

Cultivation
All mints prefer a sunny position and a moist free-draining soil and need to be watered in hot, dry periods. Other than that they are little trouble except that they will invade neighboring space if not contained. Plant them in an old bucket or bowl with sufficient drainage, or divide them with bricks or tiles at ground level. Mint rust can be a problem, so if the leaves wilt and orange spots begin to appear on the leaves, the plant should be stripped of its leaves and these consigned to the bonfire. Propagate by root or stem cuttings.

Uses

Use culinary mints when boiling potatoes and peas or as a mint sauce or jelly with lamb. Chop them into salads or add to drinks such as tea, mint julep and summer punches. Peppermint, fresh or dried, makes the classic tea for soothing troubled stomachs or head colds. Commercially it is used as a flavoring in confectionery, toothpaste and medicines. Apple and Eau de Cologne mints can be chopped and added to salads and desserts but have less flavor, although they can be used in pot pourris. Corsican mint is used to make creme-de-menthe.

Mint: An essential for the culinary herb garden, but its growth should be restricted otherwise it will swamp its neighbors.

Opposite: Nasturtium: A cheerful, easy-to-grow annual with leaves rich in vitamin C and edible flowers.

MUGWORT
ARTEMISIA VULGARIS

A herb more interesting than good looking, mugwort is related to the more commonly grown wormwood. It is a bushy shrub that grows to about 3ft (1m) with dark green leaves that are downy and silvery underneath and borne on purplish stems. The flowers are insignificant.

Cultivation
Mugwort will tolerate most positions except deep shade, but prefers a light soil. Propagate by root division in winter, or stem cuttings and seed in spring.

Uses
Mugwort was formerly used to flavor beer, a sprig being put into the mug and left to stand for a short while. It was a substitute for tea and is still used in forcemeats for pork and duck. Medicinally, small doses were used as a tonic, to cure tapeworms and to treat epilepsy. Mugwort in a hot bath acts as a deodorant and insect repellent.

Mugwort: A good foil for other herbs, mugwort is closely related to wormwood and a good addition to the herb garden for its historical uses alone.

Opposite: Orris: An early flowering iris with pure white flowers, the powdered dried roots are used as a fixative in pot pourris.

NASTURTIUM
TROPAEOLUM MAJUS

The bright trumpet-like yellow and orange flowers and sprawling habit of this traditional annual are familiar to most gardeners, as is the peppery taste of the leaves, petals and seeds.

Cultivation
Sow seeds in open ground; wait until frost danger has passed. Poor soil suits nasturtiums best as high fertility creates more leaves at the expense of flowers. Nasturtiums need no care except a watchful eye for black fly and cabbage white caterpillars.

Uses
Add to salads or pickle the seeds when green and use as capers.

ORRIS
IRIS FLORENTINA

An iris with greyish leaves and exquisitely scented flowers of the purest white appearing in early spring, orris is the perfect white garden plant.

Cultivation
Orris demands sun and prefers a well-drained soil. The rhizome roots can be divided just after flowering.

Uses
Dried and powdered orris root is used as a base in perfume and as a fixative in pot pourris.

OREGANO
OREGANUM VULGARE

This highly aromatic herb is sometimes known as wild marjoram.

Cultivation
Oregano should be planted in spring in well-drained ordinary soil in a sunny and preferably sheltered position.

Uses
Oregano is a kitchen favorite, used in meats and salads.

PARSLEY
Petroselinum crispum

The fresh curly crisp leaves of parsley must be familiar to everyone as a garnish in any restaurant if not the garden. It is an annual, but a successional sowing will provide fresh parsley for most of the year.

Cultivation

There are many superstitions about growing parsley, mostly derived from its notoriously slow and sometimes random germination. There are endless folk remedies but the answer is always use fresh seed from a reputable nursery. Sow it in shallow drills where they are intended to grow, thinning to 6in (15cm) between each plant as the seedlings appear. Begin sowing in early spring.

Uses

Fresh leaves can be added to innumerable dishes, brewed as a tea or used to make a passable wine. But parsley is a diuretic, so do not drink too much of either!

PENNYROYAL
Mentha pulegium

A small-leaved member of the mint family with purple spikes of flowers. A good groundcover plant, or for filling in cracks in paths, there is both a creeping and upright variety.

Opposite: Although previously grown as a medicinal herb, parsley is now almost exclusively grown for the kitchen.

Right: This creeping variety of pennyroyal is ideal for planting as a lawn or as groundcover between paving stones where it survives being walked on

Opposite: Rosemary: A classic herb that fits in anywhere in the garden, rosemary is here seen growing with self-seeded honesty, *Lunaria annua*.

Cultivation
Maintain as other mints.

Uses
Its English country name is 'pudding grass' as it was used in the making of black puddings. The Pilgrim Fathers took it to America to make a sleep-inducing tea and added to a bath it has a stimulating effect. It is a natural insect repellent and its Latin name meaning flea is proof of its effectiveness.

ROSEMARY
ROSMARINUS OFFICINALIS

Rosemary is a must for all herb gardens and good for a low-growing hedge or planted near a path so every time you brush against it the highly aromatic scent is released. An evergreen, with spikey leaves and misty blue flowers in spring, rosemary is not always hardy in cold, wet and frost-prone situations so should be planted in a sheltered spot. There are several varieties, one of which will match your purpose and needs.

Cultivation
Full sun and a well-drained soil are the closest rosemary can get to its natural home on the barren cliffs of Sicily, and it will thrive well in coastal areas. Propagate by taking cuttings of new growth with a heel of old wood. Pot up in a good potting compost.

Uses
Rosemary and lamb combine together so well that it is hard to think of one without the other, but it also makes a good companion to sausages and steak. It is the base for many natural beauty products, including hair rinses, bath oils and various face creams. A natural for pot pourris.

RUE
RUTA GRAVEOLENS

Grown mostly for the decorative effect of its mounds of finely cut blue-green foliage, rue is a friendly perennial which stays evergreen in most regions. It will make a good internal hedge and although tolerant of most situations flourishes in sun and a free-draining soil. The yellow flowers add little to its attractiveness and the very pungent aroma from its leaves is often unpleasant to some people. A favorite variety is 'Jackman's Blue' which is mean with flowers, but stunning with its steely-blue-tinged foliage. A variegated variety is also available.

Cultivation

Rue will take shade but revels in sun. Propagate by taking cuttings of young shoots in early summer. When placed in a suitable potting compost they will root quickly.

Uses

Although a herb with no culinary use, and poisonous if taken in large quantities, rue has long historical associations with magic. A long-held belief was that arrows, and later shot from early flintlock guns, boiled in rue water were guaranteed to hit their mark. The symbol of clubs on playing cards was derived from the shape of its leaves.

Rue: Grown mostly for its evergreen bluish foliage, rue is of no culinary value but was a medicinal herb for centuries believed to protect the user from the plague.

SAGE
SALVIA OFFICINALIS

There are many varieties of sage available to the herb gardener, all exhibiting the same characteristics of being perennial low-growing evergreen bushes that can be use as specimen plants, hedges, part of a bedding scheme or mixed border. The purple

Sage: An essential herb for the cook and gardener alike, being available in all kinds of different foliage and flower colors. This is the decorative variety 'Purpurescens'.

Opposite: Salad burnet: Although distinguished by its odd-looking knots of flowers, salad burnet is grown for the cucumber taste of its leaves.

flower spikes are an added bonus. Common sage, *S. officinalis*, has downy grey-green leaves, but the variety 'Purpurescens' has a handsome purple hue and 'Tricolor' particolored pink, white, green and purple leaves. For more variety try pineapple sage *S. rutilans*, with its bright red flowers and subtle pineapple scent from its leaves.

Cultivation
A Mediterranean plant, sage prefers sun and good drainage, but is tolerant of a wide range of sites. It is hardy, but can suffer in cold wet winters. Clipping will improve the quality of the foliage but at the expense of the delightful flowers. Propagate by stem cuttings, taking new shoots just below a leaf joint and potting up in a good potting compost. Sage is apt to become straggly after three or four years and plants may need to be replaced.

Uses
Essential for forcemeats, sausage-making and mixing with other herbs, sage will also make a refreshing tea from either fresh or dried leaves.

SALAD BURNET
SANGUISORBA MINOR

A decorative evergreen perennial with soft green leaves And unusual 'knobbly' green flowers tinged with red on elegant 1ft (30cm) stalks, salad burnet is an interesting if not showy addition to the herb garden. It is grown for its leaves which have a cucumber-like taste.

Cultivation
An easy-going plant that tolerates almost all conditions but appreciates sun. It will self-seed but seeds sown where you want them to grow are the best option.

Uses
Chop young leaves into salads or add to vinegars. Like borage they can be added to wine and summer fruit cups. In former times it was one of the healing herbs and generally used to stop bleeding.

SAVORY
(SUMMER) *SATUREJA HORTENSIS*, (WINTER) *S. MONTANA*

The two savories are very different in lifestyle, but similar in their use. Summer savory is a 1ft (30cm)-high annual with small, narrow green leaves and even smaller pink flowers in summer. Winter savory is a short evergreen shrub with spikes of mauve flowers in summer, resembling a well-fed thyme. It is amenable to clipping and can be used for low dividing hedges in the herb garden.

Above: Summer savory: The annual savory that is added to soups, stews and other meat dishes and is a good bee plant, too.

Opposite: Winter savory: This shrubby perennial savory can be clipped into a low hedge for dividing the herb garden or harvested to add its warm spicy taste to any dish that requires it.

Cultivation

Both savories relish sun and well-drained, even poor, soil. Propagate summer savory from seed, either sown in trays in early spring or directly into open ground later. Winter savory also grows from seed easily or take stem cuttings of young side shoots with a heel of old wood in summer, pot and protect for planting out the following spring.

Uses

In the kitchen both savories are best with beans, although their rather unusual flavor can add something to other vegetables, eggs, fish - especially trout - and meatloaves and sausages. The other common name is beanherb, as it not only reduces blackfly if planted close to broad beans, but also reduces flatulence.

Above: Soapwort – the undisciplined piles of pink blossoms make soapwort a good traditional cottage garden plant.

Opposite: *Artemis* are good greyish green-foliaged plants which can act as a background foil to their more colorful neighbours

SOAPWORT
SAPONARIA OFFICINALIS

A true cottage garden plant in that it is rather floppy dull green leaves and heads of campion-like pink flowers in summer. Originally grown for the soap substitute yielded by the leaves, soapwort also revels in the country name of 'Bouncing Bet'. It is an invasive plant and hard to keep in bounds, always bouncing back.

Cultivation
Any soil and a sunny position is suitable. Lift and divide plants in autumn or winter or sow from seed in early spring, potting up when the seedlings are large enough to handle and plant out in early summer.

Uses
The foliage makes a very fine soap and has been used since the sixteenth century. Today, conservators of historic tapestries and other treasured cloths use the same 'soap' for cleaning.

Opposite: Sweet cicely: A fragrant plant with an anise-like flavor ideal for the informal natural garden.

SORREL
RUMEX ACETOSA

The selected garden variety of the wild sorrel, garden sorrel is a 1.5ft (45cm) vigorous perennial with broad spear-shaped leaves which are bright green with reddish tinges. The flowers are rather uninteresting and should be pinched out to increase the output of leaves.

Cultivation
An easy-to-grow herb tolerating most soils, sorrel can be increased by division in early spring or raised from seed sown in open ground in late spring. Unless your aim is to become a snail and slug farmer use pellets to repel the beasts.

Uses
Always use sorrel fresh. The leaves make excellent soups and sauces, can be chopped to add to salads or cooked as a vegetable like spinach. But beware too much, because like rhubarb the leaves contain oxalic acid and can be dangerous in large quantities.

SOUTHERNWOOD
ARTEMISIA ABROTANUM

A shrubby herbaceous perennial with musky scented fine greyish leaves borne directly on the woody stems. It grows to about 2ft (60cm), dying back in winter. The flowers are dull and can be trimmed back if the bush is employed as a low hedge.

Cultivation
Sun and a well-drained soil match its native conditions of southern Europe and it is best treated as a herbaceous plant, cutting back all or half of the growth in spring. Propagate in early summer by cutting off the current soft stems with a heel of old wood. Overwinter in a cold frame for planting out the following spring.

Uses
A pleasant fragrant herb, southernwood can be added to pot pourris or as an insect repellent substitute for moth balls in cupboards and drawers. Its English country name of 'lad's love' reflects the belief that it was an aphrodisiac and promoted the growth of beards in adolescents, while its alternative name of 'maid's ruin' bears witness to its ability to restore hair to older balding men. There is no guarantee of either.

SWEET CICELY
MYRRHIS ODORATA

A bushy fern-like perennial which grows to about 3ft (1m) with umbels of white flowers in summer that develop into long seed pods. Dying down in winter, it emerges again in very early

spring. The whole plant exudes a perfume of aniseed mixed with celery.

Cultivation

Happy in any soil but preferring sun, sweet cicely needs little care. It can be propagated by seed or root division if required, but one sweet cicely is usually enough as it can be hard to eradicate if the colony spreads too far.

Uses

Added to salads or acid fruits it reduces tartness and adds a subtle aniseed flavor. The leaves can be eaten raw straight from the plant and are claimed to help indigestion. Commercially the seeds are added to Chartreuse liquers. It is another must for the bee garden.

TANSY
TANACETUM VULGARE

A perennial of up to 3ft (1m) with dark green fern-like leaves and heads of golden button flowers, tansy has a rather bitter smell. An attractive addition to the border for flowers in late summer.

Cultivation

Tansies are tough individuals and will grow anywhere, gradually colonising areas via its creeping rootstock. It should be treated like mint with dividers of tiles or bricks to stop it swamping its neighbours. Needless to say, it can be propagated by root division as well as by seed - neither of which will be necessary.

Uses

Once used to flavor the traditional Lenten tansy cakes, it imparts such a bitter taste that surely no-one enjoyed them. It is good for flower arranging, either fresh or dried, and makes an air freshener and insect repellent against ants, flies and moths. The flowers yield a yellow dye to wool. In the United States it is illegal to sell tansy as it is on the dangerous drugs list. So beware of eating any part of it.

TARRAGON
ARTEMISIA DRACUNCULUS

Another essential for the culinary herb garden, tarragon is an unispiring herb to look at, with narrow leaves carried on stems of about 2ft (60cm). It rarely flowers. If your tarragon is more vigorous and flowers then it is the impostor Russian tarragon,

Tarragon – useful rather than attractive, tarragon provides the kitchen with an irresistible flavor for chicken, sauces, soups and vinegar.

A.dracunculoides, which has virtually no flavor and is best abandoned and replaced with the true French tarragon.

Cultivation
Choose a sunny well-drained sheltered spot as tarragon does not like to get its feet too wet in winter. Root division in late autumn or stem cuttings from the new shoots are the preferred method of propagation. After the plant has died down in late autumn it can be cut right back to ground level.

Uses
Only use tarragon fresh, adding chopped leaves to flavor chicken, fish, eggs and salads. It is one of the *fines herbes* and a classic sauce ingredient. Leaves added to wine vinegar and left for a month in a warm place will produce your own tarragon vinegar.

Tansy – the long-lasting yellow flowers can be dried and are perfect for flower arranging.

THYME
THYMUS SPP

There are so many different thymes that a whole book and a lifetime could be dedicated to them. In reality two thymes - common thyme *T. vulgaris*, and lemon thyme, *T. citriodorus* - are familiar plants of the garden. Common thyme forms an 8in-high (20cm) mound of small-leaved aromatic foliage and is covered with clusters of pink flowers that fill with bees in summer. Lemon thyme is slightly larger-leaved that its common cousin and has a distinct lemon smell to its foliage. The variety

Common thyme: A universal herb for the kitchen, thyme's masses of flowers soon fill with tumbling bees in summer.

'Aureus' has golden leaves and is one of the best decorative plants for any garden. There are also orange-scented versions, dwarf varieties that sit snugly between paving stones and many more to discover.

Cultivation

Warm sun and a well-drained soil suit thymes best and a severe winter can lead to leaf fall. If this happens cut back the damaged growth in spring. Propagate by stem cuttings, using young shoots with a heel of old wood. Plants can be put out when large enough to handle easily.

Uses

Fresh or dry, thyme is used in a wide variety of dishes, particularly meats and in forcemeats, soups, stews and as a speciality butter and cheese. A tea is a good antiseptic mouthwash and a good all round relief for sore throats and colds.

WOAD
ISATIS TINCTORIA

A plant that yields a blue dye from its bluish-green leaves, woad is a biennial and related to the cabbage. The first year sees a growing clump of leaves, followed the next summer by 3ft-high (1m) leafy stems carrying yellowish flowers.

Cultivation

Sow seeds in late spring where you want the plants to grow, thinning as necessary to avoid overcrowding.

Uses

The blue dye was used by Ancient Britons to paint their bodies in battle, and until the beginning of this century it was an important commercial crop before the advent of artificial dyes. Recently, improved versions have been reintroduced to the farms of Europe as the demand for natural dyes has increased.

WOODRUFF
ASPERULA ODORATA

A short 8in-high (20cm) perennial that forms wonderful carpets of groundcover, woodruff has vivid green foliage studded with white star flowers in late spring.

Cultivation

Although a woodland plant and tolerant of full and partial shade, it is equally at home in the open if the soil is moist. Sow seeds in open ground in spring or lift and divide the roots during the dormant season.

Uses

Cut woodruff as it flowers and it releases a sweet new-mown hay scent, so was used to strew floors in times past. A tea from

both leaves and flowers also releases the delicious scent and is said to be good for stomach upsets.

WORMWOOD
ARTEMISIA ABSINTHIUM

A silver-foliaged perennial shrub with small yellow flowers, wormwood grows to about 3ft (1m), sometimes to 4ft (1.3m) if conditions are right. One of the best silver plants to act as a foil to other flowers, it has a typical bitter wormwood scent that keeps insects away.

Cultivation
Wormwood will grow in most soils, seeming to enjoy poor soils if in the open, and prefers sun although it will tolerate shade. It spreads by creeping rhizomes - or underground stems - which can be divided in winter.

Uses
Formerly used as a cure for worms and still used to flavor vermouths and cordial drinks, wormwood was the active ingredient in the drink absinthe until it was banned when proved to be poisonous to long-term drinkers.

Woad: A member of the cabbage family with yellow summer flowers, woad produces a blue dye.

Overleaf: Woodruff: A groundcover plant that tolerates shade, woodruff produces a scent of new-mown hay when cut and dried.

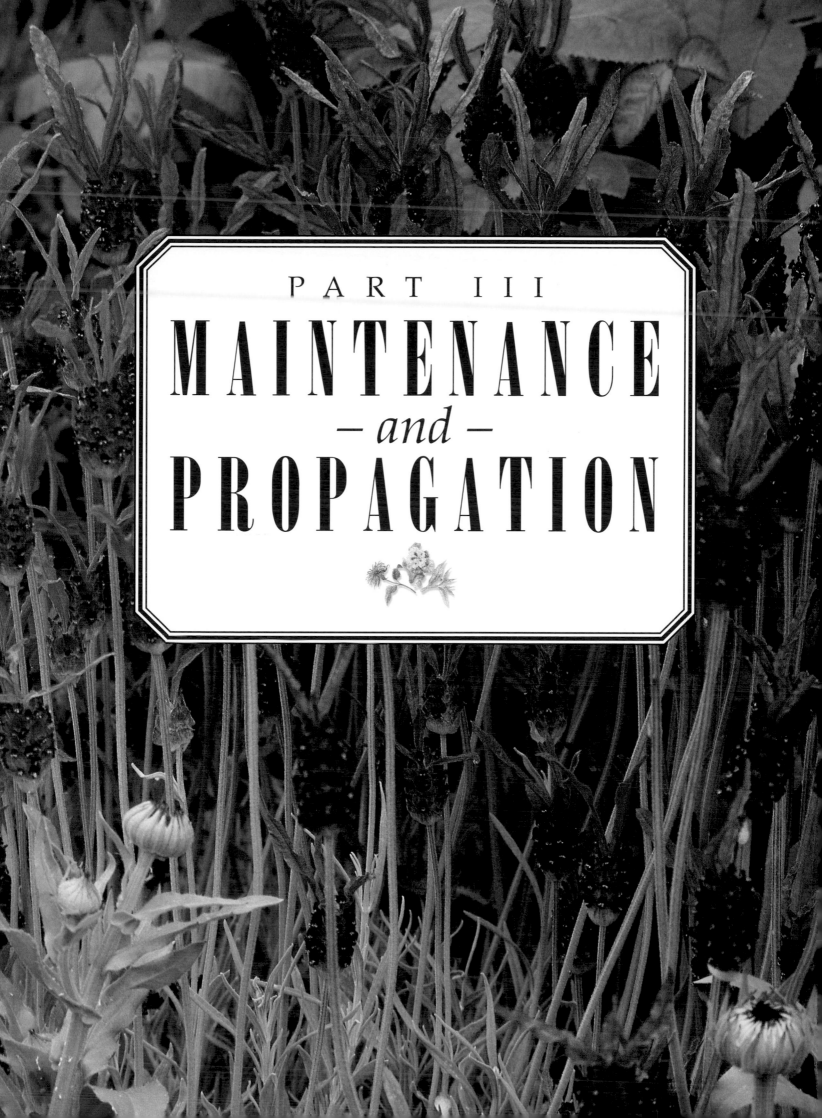

PART III
MAINTENANCE
– and –
PROPAGATION

GETTING STARTED

Herbs generally are the ideal low-maintenance plants for the garden. They need no complicated pruning, no really special way of preparing the site and they are relatively disease and pest resistant. Once you have a particular herb they are easy to propagate by different methods from sowing seed to root division and layering. Good garden practice of weeding and clearing debris is the way to keep the herb garden healthy.

The best way to start off your herb garden is to have a friend who will give you the plants you want. This has the advantage of cheapness and of establishing the garden quickly. Failing that, a visit to any garden center will provide you with a good initial choice of popular herbs, but if you want something out of the ordinary you will need to find a specialist herb nursery. Spring and autumn are the best time to plant new herbs as they transplant better when they are not in flower

When buying potted herbs there are certain things to look out for to ensure that you have a healthy specimen. Make sure that there are no damaged or dead leaves or stems on the plants and the growth is even and fresh. At the other end check that the roots are not growing out of the bottom of the pot as this indicates that it has been too long in a too small container and growth has been stunted. Equally, if the plant has only recently been potted up it will not have had enough time to establish a good root system. Check this by tapping the side of the pot to see if the potting compost is loose - a sign that it has only recently been potted.

Check for pests by inspecting the undersides of the leaves, especially for red spider mite and whitefly which can infect some plants that have been grown on in greenhouses. Any discolored leaves or mottling suggests that there may be a virus.

CONTROLLING PESTS AND DISEASES

Generally, herbs remain free from pests and diseases as the aromatic oils in their stems, flowers and leaves have a bacteriacidal and insect repellent effect. And the effect covers the entire garden, too, with strong smelling herbs providing a measure of protection to their more vulnerable neighbours.

This is just as well, because many herbs are grown to be eaten and using chemicals to protect them makes it inadvisable to use them in the kitchen until at least two weeks after they have been sprayed.

SLUGS AND SNAILS

In wet or damp weather slugs and snails spend their nighttime grazing on soft-fleshed plants. One way to deter them is to pick them off by hand and remove them to another part of the garden, but this is time-consuming and a never-ending task. Slug pellets are the answer, sprinkled around the plants. If, however, you have pets it is best to make little piles of them and hide them under a propped up tile. Good garden practice of cleaning up all dead foliage before it rots and the removal of annual weeds also makes the area less attractive to the animals.

GREENFLY, BLACKFLY AND WHITEFLY

All the aphids are a nuisance as they suck the sap from leaves and stems, causing considerable damage. In the early life of a herb systemic insecticides - those that are taken in by the plant and into the sap - can work well, but this is unsuitable if you want to harvest your herbs. The old remedy of spraying with soapy water and rubbing off the survivors does work but needs to be repeated almost daily. A few thousand ladybirds also helps! An insecticide based on pyrethrum is the best answer as this kills on contact and it is safe to harvest the plants within two days. But whichever chemicals you use always follow the manufacturer's instructions.

Snails and slugs can be troublesome in the herb garden if you allow too much debris and dead foliage to accumulate.

CATERPILLARS

Voracious caterpillars can quickly decimate a crop, especially of such annual herbs as nasturtiums, basil, sweet marjoram and summer savory. It is possible to control them by picking them off by hand, but dusting with derris powder is the most effective, although this does also kill beneficial insects such ladybirds and bees.

Rosemary and sweet cicely are sometimes infected by cuckoo spit, which is a tiny insect that sucks the sap and throws up a protective covering of white froth. These should be picked off by hand when they appear in early spring.

RUSTS AND MILDEW

Mint rust is a fungus that starts in the roots and spreads to the leaves, forming brown blotches. The only remedy is to dig up the entire plant, burn it and plant new stock in a different place. Mildew is another fungus which causes a grey mould to appear on the leaves of plants, especially sweet cicely and bergamot. The usual remedy is to dust with sulphur.

From time to time other garden pests will attack herbs, but this is rarely the case. If you can identify the culprit a good proprietary remedy should be available.

MAKING MORE HERBS

ANNUAL AND BIENNIAL HERBS THAT CAN ONLY BE GROWN FROM SEED

Ambrosia
Angelica
Anise
Basil
Borage
Caraway
Chervil
Clary sage
Coriander
Dill
Fennel
Marigold
Nasturtium
Parsley
Salad burnet
Summer savory

Making new plants from old ones is one of the great joys and satisfactions of gardening. Annuals need to be re-sown each year and you can collect your own seed to do this. Plants such as lavender which grow straggly and unkempt with age need to be replaced every few years and what is a better way to do it than to create new offspring from the parent? Just simply increasing your stock to design hedges and mass plantings comes cheaper if you use your own resources. And propagating your own plants is not difficult to do. There may appear to be complex procedures on the route to success, but think like a plant. All a seed wants to do is to grow, every cutting wants to take root so we as gardeners have only to help it - we cannot make it do it.

Every gardening book you read will have chapters on propagation and increasing your herb stock follows exactly the same principles as for any other plant. There are three major ways of doing this - sowing seeds, taking stem cuttings and by division of the roots - plus a few oddities specific to particular plants. Each entry in the A-Z gives the best method of propagation for that particular plant, this section is concerned only with principles.

SOWING SEEDS INDOORS

Early spring is the time to sow most seeds, the art being to raise plants that will be strong enough to be planted outside as soon as the weather has warmed up sufficiently and the danger of frosts is over. There is no point sowing earlier as you will have rather leggy plants when the time comes to plant them out.

The only equipment you need is seed trays, a good seed compost - never garden soil - and a newspaper. A greenhouse is a luxury and a window sill will be sufficient for most purposes. Fill the tray with compost to just below the rim and tap the base of the tray on a hard surface to settle it down. Firm the edges with your fingers and water with a fine rose about an hour before you sow. Small seeds can be scattered across the surface, larger ones sown individually at regular intervals, but no more than about twenty in each tray.

Cover the seeds with seed compost to a depth of twice their diameter and lightly water with a fine rose, making sure that

By clipping and training, cotton lavender
can be turned into a huge variety of different
designs and shapes.

you do not wash the compost off the seeds. Cover with a newspaper and keep in a warm place away from direct sunlight. It is
the combination of warmth and moisture that helps the seed to
germinate and most herb seeds germinate best in the dark.
Once the seedlings appear, however, they need light to grow so
remove the newspaper and place the tray on a window sill or in
the greenhouse. Water when the compost looks like it might dry
out, preferably by standing the trays in a bowl of water rather
than from the top.

As the seedlings grow they will become very crowded, so
once they are large enough to handle - usually when the first
true leaves begin to emerge - it is time to thin them out. Tease
the seedlings from the compost with a spatula or table fork and
replant them in another seed tray filled with a potting compost
of the same kind as the seed compost. Always handle the
seedlings by the seed leaves, not the roots stem or true leaves as
this causes irreparable damage to the young plant. Large plants
can be transplanted to individual pots if required.

HARDENING OFF

The time eventually comes when it is time to plant out your
new herbs and this is a dangerous time for them. The aim is to
gradually wean them away from the warmth and security of

the greenhouse or window sill and acclimatise them to the real outside world. This gradual process is termed hardening off. A cold frame is ideal. Place the trays of plants in the frame and over a period of weeks increase the ventilation by progressively raising the lid until it can eventually removed in warm weather. The frame can be fully closed at night. If you do not have a cold frame the trays can be put out during the day and taken in at night or alternatively improvise a cover of canes and plastic sheeting to cover the plants at night, removing it during the day. After three or four weeks, as the weather warms up, the plants are ready to take up their position in the garden.

SOWING SEEDS OUTDOORS

Some seeds are best sown directly outdoors as they do not respond well to being moved. The soil should be well dug over and preferably allowed to have the ravages of frost work on it early in the year. Rake the soil to a fine tilth and lightly water before you sow. Scatter the seeds where you want them to grow and lightly rake them in, again to about twice the depth of their diameter. As they grow make sure that they are well-watered in dry weather. The only other job is to thin them out when they are large enough to handle, spacing them apart so that when fully grown their leaves will just be touching. Thinned seedlings are not really suitable for transplanting elsewhere so they should be consigned to the bonfire or compost heap.

HERBS FROM ROOT DIVISION

This is no doubt the easiest way of increasing your herb stock. In winter, when growth has stopped dig up the whole plant making sure not to damage the roots. Shake off the soil and pull the roots apart with your hands. If it is a big plant, use two garden forks back to back to lever the rootball apart. Generally it is `best to choose the roots from around the outside of the plant, as these are younger and stronger, and discard the centre portion. Then plant the new sections of roots where you wish. Indeed, some plants will need to be divided regularly as they do grow unevenly, often with the centre dying away.

HERBS FROM CUTTINGS

Stem cuttings taken in summer are a quick way of producing new plants. Some can be taken in early summer using the new soft growth, others a little later when the stems have matured more. The optimum time is indicated for each plant in the A-Z section.

The basic principle is to use a sharp knife and take cuttings just below a leaf joint at a node on the stem as this is where the most active cells are located. Cuttings should be about 3in (7.5cm) long and the lower leaves should be stripped away. Some herbs, such as lavender, benefit from having a heel of the old wood stripped away with the cutting.

Dip the exposed cut stem in a rooting hormone and pot up in a suitable cutting compost in pots or trays. Several cuttings can be put around the edge of the pot where they seem happier

Opposite: Clipped box, cotton lavender and lavender are preferred plants for a knot garden.

HERBS GROWN FROM ROOT DIVISION

Bergamot
Catmint
Chives
Comfrey
Costmary
Elecampane
Feverfew
Lemon balm
Marjoram
Mint
Mugwort
Sage, pineapple
Savory, winter
Sweet cicely
Tansy
Tarragon
Thyme
Woodruff

**HERBS THAT
REPRODUCE BY
OFFSETS
AND RUNNERS**
Bergamot
Chamomile
Mint
Tansy
Tarragon

than in the middle. Cuttings now need warmth and moisture. A polythene bag or large jar placed over the pot will keep the cuttings in a humid atmosphere, but make sure the polythene does not touch the foliage by making a supporting frame of canes or wires. Shrubby plants like rosemary and lavender with hard needle-like leaves do not need to be kept in a humid environment so can be left in a warm, slightly shady position. Depending on the herb, roots can develop within a couple of weeks or it can take a few months. Some can be planted out the same season, others need to be overwintered in a cold frame and bay really needs two seasons before taking its chance in the outside world.

ROOT CUTTINGS

Some plants can be propagated by root cuttings, which is somewhat a cross between stem cuttings and root division. The whole plant has to be lifted and roots with new shoots identified. These can be cut off with a sharp knife and potted up in a suitable compost and the parent plant replanted.

LAYERING

Layering allows you take make new plants without disturbing the parent. Choose a side stem that is growing close to the ground and bend it over and peg part of it down into a prepared hole. Bury it with soil and keep watering throughout summer and by autumn roots should have developed. The offspring can be cut away from its parent and transferred to another part of the garden. Successful propagating cannot be guaranteed every time, so do not despair if all your plants do not all take. But it is prudent to begin to propagate more plants than you need to account for failures. And if you have no failures you have perfect presents for friends.

MAINTAINING YOUR HERB GARDEN

Once your herb garden is established there is regular work to be done to keep it in trim and healthy, but no more so than any other kind of garden. Annual weeds can be controlled by weeding by hand or hoeing and provide the opportunity to get close to your plants to remove any dead leaves or damaged shoots. Mulching with peat, wood bark or garden compost helps to keep the weeds down and traps the moisture underneath its insulating layer. Mulching with gravel or pea shingle also helps

HERBS THAT CAN BE LAYERED
Bay
Cotton lavender
Curry plant
Rosemary
Sage
Thyme

to control weeds and preserve moisture and many herbs who are native to stony soils look attractive growing out it.

Perennial weeds are, however, a major problem and before planting your herb garden it is essential to kill off as many as possible. Weedkillers when your herbs are established are difficult to apply without affecting your fresh supply of herbs. It is, however, possible to find selective weedkillers for some persistent perennials so check with your garden center.

PRUNING

Prune all shrubby herbs in spring to keep them in shape and in bounds and it helps to promote vigorous young growth throughout summer. Formal plantings, and shaped shrubs such as bay, box, cotton lavender, will need to be clipped regularly throughout summer to maintain their form, but clipping should stop in late summer to leave some leafy growth to protect the plants from winter winds and frost.

FERTILIZING

Most herbs grow better if the soil is poor and feeding them too many nutrients will make them sappy or encourage them to produce leaves at the expense of flowers. Obviously some herbs, such as sorrel and basil, are grown for their leaves and may benefit from a dressing of slow-release organic fertilisers such as bonemeal. But a supply of garden compost from the compost heap will probably be enough to keep all your herbs happy. Other than these, and regular tasks such as watering, the herb garden will look after itself. Again, good garden hygiene of clearing away debris and dead foliage to discourage pests and diseases should be maintained throughout the year. The only job left is to spend time in your garden, enjoying the various fragrances and the rainbow of colours that it will provide.

WHEN TO PLANT

Herbs can be planted in spring or autumn, just before growth starts or as the plant become dormant for the winter. Autumn planting is fine if the herb has developed a good root system over the summer, but not suitable for ones that have not and they should be overwintered in their pots.

Annuals can be sown out of doors in early spring, or if seed-grown indoors planted out in late-spring as long as the danger of frost has passed.

HERBS PRUNED IN SPRING

A hard pruning encourages strong new growth.

Southernwood
Wormwood

HERBS THAT SHOULD BE CUT BACK AFTER FLOWERING

Cotton lavender
Curry plant
Hyssop
Lavender
Rosemary
Sage
Thyme

INDEX

PICTURE CREDITS

Garden Picture Library: GPL/Steven Wooster: 19, 83; GPL/Mel Watson: 25; GPL/John Glover: 26, 36, 38, 45; GPL/Lynne Brotchie: 27; GPL/Bob Challinor: 32; GPL/PW Flowers: 33; GPL/Mayer/Le Scanff: 34, 59; GPL/Linda Burgess: 35 (bottom), 41, 47, 52, 53, 70; GPL/JS Sira: 48/49, 135; GPL/Henk Dijkman: 51; GPL/Roger Hyan: 54/55; GPL/Christel Rosenfeld: 56; GPL/Erika Craddock: 57; GPL/Clive Boursell: 62; GPL/Chris Burrows: 63; GPL/Vaughan Fleming: 64; GPL/Michael Howes: 65; GPL/Brigette Thomas: 137; GPL/Jerry Parva: 138.

Michael Janulewicz: 8.

Garden Matters: 9, 10, 11, 12, 14, 18, 20, 22/23, 24, 46, 60, 61, 66, 67, 69, 71, 74, 75, 76, 77, 78, 79, 80, 81, 82, 84, 85, 87, 89, 91, 92, 93, 95, 96, 97, 98, 100, 101, 103, 103, 105, 107, 109, 110, 110, 111, 113, 114, 115, 117, 118, 119, 121, 122, 123, 124, 125, 127, 128, 129, 130, 131, 132.

Clive Nichols: 7, 15, 16/17, 21. 29/29, 30, 42. 73, 133.

Reed International Books: RIB/Melvin Grey: 35 (top), 37, 39; RIB/David Jordan: 40.

We would also like to thank the owners of the following gardens and the various garden designers who kindly allowed Clive Nichols to photograph their work: Chiping Croft, Glos, 15; Sticky Wicket, Dorset, Pam Lewis, 16/17; Herb Farm, Sonning, Oxfordshire, Richard Scott, 21; Joan Murdy, 28/29; Nuala Hancock & Mathew Bell, 30; Julie Toll, 42.